Digital Dollars and Cents

A Virtual CFO's Playbook to help Digital Companies Create a Financial Roadmap to Success

Digital Dollars and Cents
© 2017 by ASG Publications

Published by ASG Publications
Fort Wayne, IN
SummitCPA.net

Cover Design by Wilhelm Design

First Printing: November, 2017

Table of Contents

Acknowledgements

A whopping and full-hearted THANK YOU to my wife, April, for hanging with me all these years through both the successes and, more importantly, failures, and for the sacrifices she has endured to help push our business forward.

Wayne Gretzky once said, "A good hockey player plays where the puck is. A great hockey player plays where the puck is going to be." With that said, I'd like to thank my business partner and great friend, Adam Hale, for taking a chance with me and helping implement an innovative business strategy that's pushed people to think differently about accounting. I often look back and wonder how two whacky accountants could push the envelope as much as we have over the past years. Thank you, Adam!

I would like to thank all of our clients for their trust and loyalty over the years. I hope that our team exceeds your expectations. And, when they don't, I hope that they make things right.

I would like to specially thank the team at Lullabot who was crazy enough to hire a Virtual CFO to manage the financial health of their company in a state that was 900 miles away from their headquarters back in 2011. I would like to thank Matt Westgate, co-founder of Lullabot, for being such a great friend and mentor.

I would also like to thank the hardest working person that I have ever met, Todd Stewart. Todd is the owner of One

Resource Group, an extremely successful owner of a Brokerage General Agent or BGA for short. Todd has been a client and close friend for many years. Todd, thanks for taking a risk in allowing our team to take over the CFO responsibilities of your company. More importantly, thanks for being such a great friend.

I'd also like to thank Todd Nienkerk, co-founder of Four Kitchens, and Lori Patterson, co-founder of Pixo, both for being awesome clients, great friends, and for letting us share their thoughts in this book.

Thank you to Bureau of Digital for giving me a platform to teach business owners how to be profitable. Your camps and summits helped me find my voice and ultimately the inspiration for putting this book together. Carl Smith, I love the community that you're building in the digital industry. Thank you for letting me be a part of it. You truly are a great friend!

Finally, I'd like to thank the Summit CPA Group team. You're a family of professionals who has put up with my craziness and constant push for change on an almost daily basis. Many changes to come.

Jody Grunden
Fort Wayne, Indiana

Preface

"I love helping people succeed in business and, to me, accounting is the platform I can use to do that." - Jody Grunden

First of all, let me say thank you for actually picking up this book and beginning to read it. Hopefully you'll continue. If you do, I can promise you a couple things. First, you'll learn stuff. Important stuff. Things that will help you run your business better. Second, you won't be bored. Okay, I can't promise you that. But I can tell you the goal of this book is to provide you with important financial advice and information and do it in a way that doesn't make your eyes glaze over.

So, who am I and why am I the guy writing this book? My name is Jody Grunden, and I'm a CPA. Uh oh, I might be losing you. Yeah, I know, accountants are the most boring people on the planet. A stuffed shirt that loves numbers but has trouble with people. No one can suck the life out of a room like an accountant. But stick around because you'll see I'm not like those boring bean counters. I don't speak "accountingese." I can't remember the last time I wore a tie to work. I love helping people succeed in business and, to me, accounting is the platform I can use to do that.

I'm the co-founder and CEO of Summit CPA Group. CEO is "accountingese" for leader. I apologize for using it. Summit CPA Group was founded in Fort Wayne, Indiana, but that doesn't matter because our entire team, as well as our clients, are all over the US. We're a distributed company that works virtually with our clients – now that's a mouth full! We focus primarily on Virtual CFO Services. Companies that can't afford or don't want to hire a full-time Chief Financial Officer or Controller hire us to provide those services. We're also hired by companies that want a team of professionals taking ownership of their finances rather than just a single in-house CFO. We have clients and team members that we've never met in person. Admit it, that makes accounting seem kind of cool, doesn't it?

We started working on this concept in 2002 and took on our first virtual CFO client in 2004. That client was a typical successful business owner. In his case, he had 5 locations, each with its own set of problems. His company was humming along, not sure how they got where they were and not sure what the next move would be. We helped give him direction which gave him the ability to sleep better at night. For the first time, he knew someone was looking over the financial statements, and more importantly, looking over his future. Furthermore, we helped him build his "empire" and eventually sell his businesses for much more than what it was worth back in 2004. We lost a client the right way!

That's really what makes us different than other accounting firms. We focus on the future through forecasting. We don't just look at the past and say "Hey, here's what you did and why you did it."   We look at the past, the present, and then we help our clients look to the future.   What's coming up next? Strategic decisions like hiring employees or even worse, letting people go.   Determining which services are more profitable than others. Determining how to price a service properly.   Determining what their pipeline needs to be in order to handle cash flow over the next month, three months, year, etc. We actually look as far as up to three years in advance at all times with clients, which really helps them map out their future and set their goals.

We don't want to just predict the future, we want to help them shape it so it's the right future. It's all about informed decisions. We don't want them just sticking a finger up in the air and deciding, "Hey, I'll hire someone today because it feels right." We want to make sure they understand the consequence of doing that and the timing of everything that needs to be done in order for that to happen.

You can probably relate to our typical client. Not a financial big picture person. Just the opposite. They're great at their craft. Really great. But they don't have that strong business sense or don't want to spend the time doing it because they want to actually spend their time working in the business and helping it evolve and grow. They want somebody else to take the financial side and run with it. You'll hear from some of them in this book. They have some interesting stories to share.

We help our clients overcome their fear of the unknown. The fear of, "Do I have enough cash in the bank right now to handle the next payroll, the next two payrolls, the next three or four payrolls? Am I making the right decision in making this hire? How much should I pay this person?" Those are things that even the best businessperson may not know. That's where we come in to help and direct them, ease their pain, and give them that ability to sleep at night.

Most of our clients are under the marketing umbrella. Marketing firms, agencies, web design and development companies, SEO firms, software companies, and so on. But if you aren't in that arena, don't leave....the things I'll be talking about in this book apply to pretty much any service-based business.

We can certainly relate to the challenges and struggles our clients have faced in growing their businesses because we've been there too. We've made our share of mistakes. Ironically, for an accounting firm, probably our biggest mistake was how we priced our product. We did what many businesses do—we priced it based on how long we thought that it would take us to perform the service. Boy, did we underestimate it! That mistake really hit us hard and about put us out of business. Cash flow was tight. The line of credit maxed out. You've heard of people living "paycheck to paycheck." Well in the business world, we lived "payroll to payroll." You might be able to relate. All of a sudden owning a business wasn't fun anymore.

We knew that if we didn't do something now we would have to quickly morph from owners to employees. And, neither Adam nor I had any interest in doing that. We had to start working "on the business" instead of working "in the business".

We brought in a consultant that really helped us refocus. We developed a forecast that gave us a roadmap to success. In developing the forecast, we identified four metrics that were key to our business. Monitoring and managing these metrics really turned our business around. I will be covering these metrics with you throughout the book.

By going through this internal process, we identified that we were waaaaaay off on pricing our service. We learned we needed to price our service based on what people would pay for it. We then put it into a flat-fee model so that it was a win for both our clients _and_ for us. This was a simple change that turned our company around.

I am sharing this with you because I want to stress that even a couple of (self-proclaimed) pretty bright CPAs can struggle with creating a profitable company.

Although we do not bill hourly, we do track hours. We track them for internal purposes. After all, we are accountants, we like to know these things. We want to be able to manage our processes. So, our pricing is totally based on a flat fee structure. The cool thing about flat fee billing is that our clients do not get a bill every time they talk to us. We always thought that was a counterproductive way to run a consulting business. I told you that we are not a typical accounting firm. Our clients know what they're going to pay, and that number doesn't change. And they know we're going to be there for them. Whenever they need us. They can reach us anytime. We're not nine to five because our clients are not nine to five.

So how can we do this virtually? One word. Technology. We'll talk on the phone if we have to, but most of the time we meet face to face. Or actually, we meet webcam to webcam. We utilize web conferencing, allowing our team to have face-to-face contact with the client even though we may be all across the country. With video conferencing and screen share, the communication is very effective. It's like having someone down the hall, only you don't have to get up and walk into their office. And you don't have to waste time driving to and from meetings. Can a distributed team working virtually be effective – I can say without a doubt, "yes." Can a distributed team that works virtually with their clients be profitable? The answer again is "yes." Utilizing technology along with adjustments in pricing allowed us to really turn things around.

We work very closely with our clients. We meet with them on a regular basis, usually once a week. Some clients we meet with a couple times a week. As they work with us and get to know us, they often begin to think of us as a partner. Some have even asked us to be on their board of directors. There's no fee for that. We just do it. It gives them comfort knowing there's someone else looking over the important stuff.

We bring a ton of value to our clients. Right from the beginning, we help them set their goals. Goals based on their company culture, not ours. Who are we to say how they are supposed to run their company? Based on what those goals are, we give them the guidance or roadmap on how to reach those goals. On the way to achieving those goals, we look to reduce risk. And the biggest risk that a company faces is running out of cash. So, we may tell them, "In order to achieve the goals that you set in the timeframe that you want to achieve them, here's what we expect you to do. We want you to first generate a strong cash position, and we want you to build a cash reserve of 10% of annualized revenue." For some companies, we may tell them that we want to build a cash reserve of as much as 30%.

Think about that, and think about your revenue. A $2 million company should have $200,000 to $600,000 in cash set aside at all times. That's an eye-opener. A lot of our clients look at it and say "Whoa, that's unbelievable." But then we show them how to do it. We break it down, put the forecast together, show them what their sales pipeline needs to be in order to sustain the forecast, and then show them what they have to do in order to achieve it. Basically, we put together the roadmap for them to be successful. Then we manage it every single week, every single month, to make sure that they're on track. And if they're not, we figure out why. Not that they couldn't have done it themselves, they'd just never thought about it that way.

Now the geeky stuff about me. I love to go to work every day. I love the way we're helping business owners become more profitable. It's a cool experience. How many accountants can say that? I also love when we lose a client.

Not an unhappy one, but one who sells their business. Talk about the wow factor. We've worked with a client and brought them to a point that they never expected. We lose a client but we've made a friend forever, and that is when we've really done our job.

The end game is a big part of business strategy. If you haven't thought about that, you should. We make sure our clients do. In order to put together a proper forecast, you have to know what the end game is supposed to look like. That's another eye-opener for them.

We think it's important to give our clients a really awesome user experience. I know, meeting with your accountant isn't a party. But working with clients is fun for us, and we think it should be the same for them. We look at what we want our team to experience and what we want the client to experience, and we mesh the two together. So, when we put a team together, our team is excited to work for our company. When the client sees that, it makes them excited to work with our team.

I hear success stories all the time when I speak at seminars and conferences. Clients come up and say, "Man, your team is awesome. How'd you get such cool accountants?" Once again, let me remind you the word "cool" and the word "accountant" don't usually appear in the same sentence unless accompanied by the words "not very." But the members of our team are excited. They joke with the clients. They build a rapport and a relationship, and yes, they have fun. They become a client's friend. Your accountant, your friend. Go figure.

Introduction

"We really had no clue about the finances of our own business, which is scary." - Matt Westgate

Now that you know who I am and why I'm here, let's turn things around and ask you those same questions. But let me take a shot at how you're going to answer them. You aren't a financial expert. You're a business owner who has to deal with finances. You're good at what you do. From building websites to building buildings, you've built a successful company, assembled a good team, and you're doing good work for your clients. But you can't ignore the financial side of the business. You do have to figure out what to pay yourself and your employees. Then you have to make sure you have enough money to do that, as well as pay your mortgage or rent, your taxes, and all of the business expenses. You also need to figure out what to charge your clients, the best way for them to pay you, how profitable you are, and what to do with those profits.

That's a long list. Do you know the answers to all those questions? If you don't, you're far from alone. A lot of business owners don't. Maybe you do the books yourself. Or as the business has grown, maybe your spouse or a friend or a part-time bookkeeper has taken over that responsibility. But who looks at the big picture?

Matt Westgate, co-founder of Lullabot, told me about the bewilderment he felt around the finances in his company:

We had an internal person who was keeping an eye on our finances, and we had an external accountant. But the internal person left and we lost that visibility into our finances. My business partner and I don't have business degrees. We don't have a business background. We develop websites. We just knew that things were going well. We thought that's all we needed to pay attention to, but then when that other person left, we realized that we could barely have a conversation with our accountant. He would show us a balance sheet, and we didn't know the first thing about how to even process that ourselves. We really had no clue about the finances of our own business, which is scary. We were just looking at our bank accounts, saying, "Yeah, looks like there's some money in there, so I think we're doing well."

If you're like many business owners, you suddenly found yourself with a company doing a million dollars in annual revenue, or two million or three, with 10 to 20 employees or more, and you said to yourself, "How did I get here? I have a real company now. What do I do now?"

Todd Nienkerk, co-founder of Four Kitchens, told me about the ineptitude he felt around the financial side of things:

My business partner and I are not business people. We're not MBAs. We didn't go to business school. We're designers. We're developers. We're web people. We like to make websites. We created this organization around our passion, and our passion isn't necessarily financial planning and tax preparation and things like that. We're just not particularly good at the finance side of things.

Ask yourself another very important question: Do you know what you don't know? What you may be looking for is a barometer. Once companies hit that million-dollar mark, there's a whole new list of questions to ask: Where are we compared to similar companies? What should our net income be? What should our pricing structure be? What should our cash situation be? When should we hire or fire people?

Chances are, you've done it by your gut so far. And your gut has done pretty well for you. But you can't do it in a vacuum forever. You reach a point where you need to be sure you are where you should be, and where you want to be. What are your competitors charging clients? How are they paying their people? Have you put together a detailed forecast of the next year? Most companies don't. Many are just guessing what revenues could be like next year.

Let me tell you what happens when we meet with a new client. We ask a lot of questions, many of which they can't answer. I'll ask you the questions below. See if you can answer them. If not, you might want to think about getting more help than that part-time bookkeeper.

Todd Nienkerk:

He asked for our last 12 months of financials, and then he put together this report. It was very broad, a very high-level view of where we were compared to the overall economy, compared to people in our industry, where our biggest expenses are, and how they rank comparatively with other companies. It was data that we had never had before. That was totally new to us. We realized that what we were getting was exactly what you get when you hire a consultant of any type. You're getting perspective outside of your own organization and experience. That's what has been most valuable, I think, having a team to pull together data and trends and stuff from multiple industries or from our peers themselves to give us a much more accurate weather report about how we're doing within our peer group.

The first question we ask is how much cash you have available and how much you'll have in the next six months. Many clients know the first part, but the second part stumps them. Big time. This comes back to the forecasting I keep mentioning. You know your bank balance today, but can you project what it will be three months, six months, a year down the road?

Now that you have that deer in the headlights look, we ask about profits. What is your bottom line net profit and what should you expect to have in order to get the necessary cash on hand down the road? Again, that's a tough question to answer. Smaller companies definitely struggle with it. Bigger companies may have a better grasp because they've had to force themselves to learn it. They don't quite understand how it works, but they know the number. We dig a little deeper and determine the amount of culture hours that a company gives your team (if you're not familiar with the term "culture hours," I'll cover it in more detail in Chapter 2). We also determine the weekly billing expectation that a typical employee would have. The questioning continues as we get a better understanding of the company and its issues. Do you know what each individual producer should generate revenue-wise, and net income-wise? Do you know what the company's revenue should be based on the number of hours your team is expected to bill each year? Do you have a large enough sales pipeline in order to maintain the forecast? Do you know what your average bill rate is? Hint, it is not equal to your standard bill rate.

Then we talk about employees. How well do you want to pay them? Do you want to pay in the 90th percentile of all companies like yours and be top tier, or drop down to the 50th percentile and be the national average, or do you want to drop down to the 30th percentile and be low-cost leader? There's nothing wrong with any of those answers, by the way, as long as we consider all of the factors. Where are you located? Do your employees work in-house or remotely? What does your billing rate justify?

Next, we talk about vacations. We all like to take vacations. Let's say you want to do something nice for your employees and give everyone three weeks' vacation instead of two. That's cheaper than giving everyone raises, right? Hold on a minute. Did you really look at the numbers? You might have just accidentally taken $150,000 or more off your bottom line.

Was that a smart decision to do at this point, or should you have waited longer until you built up your cash reserve?

These are all part of your company culture. Do you have one? You do, even if you don't know what it is. Every company has one. And there's no right or wrong culture because what's right for you may not work for any other company like yours.

Lori Gold Patterson, co-founder of Pixo, on company culture:

> *I come from an engineering background, and worked in corporate America for about 10 years before my brother and I both left corporate America. While we were both very quickly climbing up the ladder, we felt that our values were not shared in the corporate environment. We were often seeing major decisions being made behind closed doors and then seeing our colleagues let go without them knowing, or strategic directions changing very quickly. We started this company to bring the value of "the human comes first" to a very cutthroat industry, the IT consulting industry. Our company culture is the base of why we went into business. It is everything to us.*

You need to know what your culture is, and how it impacts your bottom line. As I have heard my business partner Adam Hale say on several occasions, "profit is not a bad word". As business owners, we're in business to make a profit, to grow the company, and to give our team the protection and security they really need. That's all part of company culture.

Matt Westgate:

I think the biggest contribution to our culture that Summit played a role in was not making money the bad guy. There's this feeling of, "Oh no, if we open up our finances maybe people will see how greedy we are," or, "We're all doing this for fun. We're all doing this for the love of the work and not the money." In reality, it's "No, we're doing it for love, but we're doing it for money, too." We're shooting ourselves in the foot if we're not talking about the money side. Money wasn't a part of our culture. Summit's team brought a sense of financial awareness. They said, "You guys need to learn your stuff." Like, "You're running a business and you need to know the business of the business." We were able to do that, and we found our way, the Lullabot way, if you will, of bringing finance and financial awareness into the company. We couldn't have done that without Summit's guidance on just helping us get smart and helping us identify what our KPIs were and why they're important.

How much do you make a year? I know that's an uncomfortable question to ask, but we're not sitting down face to face, so let me ask it. Here's why. We expect every single company to generate at least a 10% bottom line net income and that is after paying the owner's salary. Which should be at least $150,000 a year. Most of the clients we meet with aren't making nearly that much. We don't tell them this to make them feel bad. It's to make them realize what they're missing, and how they can fix that. You're the owner. You're taking all the risks. You need the reward. If not, go work for someone else.

Lori Gold Patterson:

> *When we started as a company, my brother, who is a programmer, got paid for the hours that he could bill. Other people that we brought in could get paid. I couldn't get paid because we didn't have anybody. It took me eight years before my salary in the company matched my salary coming out of corporate America, which is a long time. The other benefits — my quality of life and work-life balance — were so much better that it was well, well worth it. Now, I am fully compensated.*

What are you charging your clients? What should you be charging your clients? Are they the same? Probably not. Realistically, I am guessing that only about 10% of your peers have a good idea of what they should be charging their clients. Just about everyone thinks they're charging the right amount. What many don't understand is what number they have to charge in order to make their business successful, which is a completely different thing. Back to employee pay for a minute. If your employees are paid in the 90th percentile but you're billing in the 50th percentile, the margin may not be big enough to cover expenses, pay taxes, and build cash.

It's funny, I have asked groups of owners at various speaking events what their standard rate is. As you could guess, their answers varied dramatically from as low as $100 an hour, to upwards of over $400 an hour. When everybody hears the rates, you can see the eyes open wide and they start thinking, "Wow, that firm charged that much? Their firm is not any more special than ours. How do they get away with that?"

Then they start justifying it, thinking it's because the other firm is in New York City or LA, and then they discover the firm is actually in the same size city as them. So how does one company charge four times as much as a similar company? It's just an expectation.

One last question for you. What type of client should you be pursuing? What size projects, what size revenue? How can you make sure you're taking on a client that will provide maximum profits? Okay, I lied, that wasn't the last question. This one is, and it directly relates to what type of client you want. What type of company are you? High quality work or crank it out quickly? High price or more bang for your buck? There's nothing wrong with any of those niches. As long as you're charging the right amount and have the right number of clients.

There's an important reason we do all this, and an important reason you should ask yourself these same questions. Don't feel bad about not knowing the answers. Believe me, owners of businesses much larger than yours can't answer them either. It's because we want people to know how important those answers are, and the impact they can have. You shouldn't have to operate in a vacuum. Because we work with so many companies like yours, we can look at your numbers and tell you where you should be. How many employees you should have based on your revenue. What your net income should be. What your expenses should be. What you should be charging. How you compare to similar companies. If you're out of balance, we look at where the problem is. Are your administrative costs too high? Are you paying too much for rent or mortgage? Are you charging enough? Where are you leaking money if you're not hitting what should be your bottom line? Those are really important things to know.

But they aren't always easy things to hear. When we look at our clients' numbers and figure out their pipeline, we can put together forecasted revenue numbers. And we can say with great certainty that it's an accurate forecast. The problem is, sometimes it's not a good forecast. Sometimes we look at it and say, "That revenue level isn't enough. Forget profits, you won't be able to cover expenses in three months." Maybe it's time to cut expenses or downsize. Or maybe it's time to increase billable hours or your standard rate. Look how many times the weather forecast changes because a storm fizzled out or changed direction. You can prevent a storm from hitting your business by making changes.

I know, I've asked you a lot of questions. Maybe you've already asked yourself most of them. But if you haven't, you should. And if you don't know the answers, get them. The future of your business is riding on this.

Chapter 1: Counting Cash

"Probably the most critical thing for my organization was that once I had the tools to look at our finances properly, I realized we had a cash flow problem." - Matt Westgate

Here's a question: How much cash do you have? Not in your wallet (although, if you're like me, you don't have a lot there, but you do have that emergency $20 bill stashed in a compartment). No, I'm talking about the cash that you have on hand in your business. How many accounts do you have, and what's in each one? And here are the important questions: Do you know which specific accounts you should have, and do you know how much you should have in each one? The answer to the second question may not just surprise you, it may change your whole way of doing business.

Let's start with the accounts — money in the bank. That means money that's available for you to use anytime you need it, money that's designated for specific purposes, and money that could, and should, be going into your pocket.

How many accounts does your business have? Chances are, you just have one. That's what many businesses have. And that's a big mistake. When we meet with new clients, one of the things we do is define three different accounts which I believe are imperative for every company to have.

1. The first one is what we call an **operating account**. That's where you have the money that will pay your payroll and your vendor bills.

2. The second one is what we call a **cash reserve account**. Which is just what it sounds like. Money that's there if you need it. The combination of the two is considered your working capital. And, the combination of the two accounts should have a pretty substantial balance.

3. The third account is your **tax reserve account**. You know you're going to have to pay taxes every quarter. Where does that money usually come from? It should come from its own account, one you contribute to regularly.

Do you have these three accounts? Or two of them? Or just one combined company account? If the answer is just one, you're far from alone. Most companies operate that way. Hopefully, after reading this chapter, you'll change that. At least after you get over the shock of learning how much you need in those accounts.

So, let's do the math. The operating capital account is easy. You need to always have two payrolls worth of cash in there. Obviously, there are a lot of bills to pay out of that account, but the payroll figure is a good balance to keep on hand here. And, it is easy to remember and to calculate on the fly. If your semi-monthly payroll is $50K per payroll, then you will want to carry approximately $100K in this account (2 payrolls x $50K per payroll).

Put your additional cash into the cash reserve account. Hopefully this account is going to earn you a little interest, so your money is actually earning you a little money instead of just sitting there, because....here comes the shocker....you need to keep a LOT of money in this account. It's your way of avoiding risk.

Just how much? Your operating account and cash reserve accounts should add up to 10-30% of your annual revenue. That's right, up to 30% of your annualized gross revenue should be in the bank at all times. That's basically two to six months worth of expenses. I'll explain the logic for determining whether your magic percent is 10% or higher in just a minute. But first, do the math. Let's say your annual revenue is $2.5 million, then you will need a minimum of $250K in the bank ($2.5 Million x 10%). Do you have that much on hand? If you're a 30-percenter, that's $750,000 ($2.5 Million x 30%). In cash. On hand. Okay, you can swallow now.

Lori Gold Patterson:

> In January of 2015, I was diagnosed with stage 4 ovarian cancer. Fortunately, I'm good now. But that was the moment in time that all CEOs dread. What happens if suddenly, with no time to plan, you're gone? My company, because of our strong values, because the whole company makes decisions together because we're very transparent, the people at Pixo have strong ownership in the company. I had no worries at all about everybody rising to the occasion. This was their moment, where they were going to make it or break it. Their culture stayed intact, our clients stayed exceptionally happy, and people were very bonded. I was gone for six months.   When I came back, everything on the surface looked fantastic, except we

had no money left in the company. They had drained our entire reserves. It didn't help that my director of operations was on maternity leave half the time I was gone. So, the only two people in the company who really understood the financials were gone, and at that time, we didn't have good executive reporting. We didn't have any regular processes or key performance indicators or anything that enabled the executive team and the company as a whole to make good decisions or to know what was coming around the bend. Before we implemented those processes, we had $349 in the bank.

Why is this so important? It's all about your cash flow, and your forecasting. Let's face it, your revenue can vary widely from month to month. If you have an accurate forecast, you'll know when you're going to have the highs and when you're going to have the lows. But your base monthly expenses are always going to be there. I should also point out when I say 10-30% of your annual revenue, we're looking at the PREVIOUS 12 months.

Cash truly makes big obstacles look small. What do I mean about that? Look at all of the obstacles that you come across in your day-to-day business. Obstacles like customers paying you late or, worse, not at all. Losing a big client. Having to give a client a refund for any reason. Having three payrolls in a month instead of two. Having a partner come up to you and decide that she would like to move on and get bought out. Having the opportunity to hire a once in a lifetime employee. You get the idea. Now let's visualize that those obstacles are boulders – yes boulders. Some may be big boulders, some may be small boulders, but none-the-less they are all boulders.

Now let's visualize that you are heading down the highway of success. What are you traveling in? Stay with me now. You have the option of heading down the highway of success with either a monster truck or a scooter. You are not in a hurry so you pick a scooter. So, now you are heading down the highway of success, getting passed by cars of all sizes, getting honked at for traveling at slow speeds, and then to your surprise, you come across all of the boulders blocking the highway. The boulders are so high that there is no way your scooter can go over them. And they extend the entire length of the highway so you cannot go around them. What are you going to do?

You may have to make a lot of course corrections. Maybe go a different direction. The wrong direction but it may be the only direction. You may not be able to go anywhere at all. Your journey may have just come to an end. Wish you would have picked the Monster truck? With the Monster truck, you could have cruised down the highway of success, stayed with traffic, and not got honked at. Oh, and by the way, what about the boulders? What boulders? Do you mean that you did not remember the boulders? The answer is "no" you don't. You generally don't remember the small stuff. You climbed over the boulders as if they were a mere bump in the road. I think you get where I am going with this. The Monster truck and the scooter represented how much cash you had in the bank.

You can guess which one I want to be driving down the highway of success. As I mentioned earlier, having cash truly makes big obstacles look small. According to the "Report on Economic Well-Being of US Households in 2016," prepared by the Board of Governors of the Federal Reserve System in 2017, 44% of Americans don't have cash or its equivalent to pay for a $400 emergency expense.[1] That, to me, is very shocking. Most American's are driving scooters. Don't let your business fall into that same trap. Drive the monster truck.

Matt Westgate:

> *Probably the most critical thing for my organization was that once I had the tools to look at our finances properly, I realized we had a cash flow problem. We*

[1] "Report on the Economic Well-Being of U.S. Households in 2016," Board of Governors of the Federal Reserve System, 2017

asked, "OK, how do we fix it?" Our virtual CFO basically said, "You guys need to do some things differently. You're thinking about money the wrong way." His primary recommendation was that we needed 10% of our revenue in the bank on a trailing 12-month basis. Look at our revenue for the last 12 months, take 10% of it, whatever that is, that needs to be in our bank. I said, "Well, we have a line of credit." He said, "Yeah, how does it feel when you dip into your line of credit?" I said, "Not very good. Not very good at all." He really wanted us to build up 10% of our revenue, and I quickly realized that that was not something I could do alone. That is a seismic shift in the organization to change that mentality, to change that way of thinking. So, at our company retreat that year, where we had everyone together, we started teaching the team about finance. We opened our books. That was one of the scariest things I've done in the company. We said, "Look, here's where we are. You know, we don't have the money in the bank that we'd like to have. We want to operate differently, we want to be different."

The third account is the tax reserve account. You're going to pay your taxes quarterly. Most companies just write a check four times a year and take the money out of their main operating account. Maybe they transfer it from a savings account. But it rarely comes from its own account. We recommend to our clients that they have at least 40% of their forecasted net income set aside in the tax reserve account. The difference between the tax account and the other accounts is this one is based on your net income, while the others are based on gross revenue. You should contribute to your tax reserve account regularly.

I'm not going to advise you on your taxes, but if you're wondering how much you should pay quarterly, here's a pretty simple formula: Take whatever your accountant figures at the end of the year and divide it by four. You use those nice little coupons they give you, and you file the minimum amount each quarter. Let the excess ride in the account to pay out when taxes are due in April.

Let's crunch some numbers. Take a company with $3.4 million in top-line revenue. Let's call their adjusted net income $655,000. Not bad. We're going to take the $655,000 and multiply it by 40%. That gives us $262,000. That's what we'll anticipate paying to Uncle Sam — some of it quarterly throughout the year and the full amount paid by April 15th. So, this company needs to transfer, over the course of the year, $262,000 into their tax reserve account. Monthly, they will transfer $21,833 ($262,000/12) into the tax reserve account. Quarterly, they will withdraw and send the quarterly estimated tax payments to the IRS. The account will grow and the difference will stay in the account until the tax return is completed and the final taxes are due.

Never count the money in your tax reserve account as working capital. It's actually a liability owed to the government. It's money that you owe, so even though it may be an account with a substantial balance, the money in that account is a substantial debt waiting to be paid.

But let's go back to the operating cash and cash reserve accounts. Let's use the same company, with its $3.4 million in revenue. And, let's also say that the company had $1.7 million in employee cost. If they're a company that should have 10% on hand, that's $340,000. If they're geared more toward 30%, the figure is $1,020,000. Or maybe they should fall somewhere in between. Let's say this company has a combined total of $526,000 in those two accounts. So, we divide $526,000 by their $3.4 million in revenue, and we get 15%. If this company should be at 30%, they're not exactly in trouble, they just do not have enough cash on hand. If they're a 10-percenter, life is good. Actually, they may have too much in there. Situations like that give the owners the opportunity to possibly pull some money out and put it in their pockets. We will call that a profit distribution.

I know I've repeated 10% and 30% several times. That's over-simplifying. There's no one-size-fits-all. Cash on hand requirements differ from company to company. But 10% is concrete. 10% should be considered a company's cash floor. I've yet to have a client that shouldn't have a minimum of 10% of revenue on hand. But there are plenty of companies where the need is 12% or 17%, or 18.5%.

WORKING CAPITAL REQUIREMENT

10%	30%
High Recurring Revenue	No Recurring Revenue
Zero Accounts Receivable Days	High Accounts Receivable Days
Strong Pipeline	Weak Pipeline
Younger Partners	Retiring Partners
Low Growth	High Growth
No big purchases in the near-term	Big purchases in near-term
One Owner	Multiple Owners
Owners have high personal liquidity	Owners have low personal liquidity
No Clients greater than 10% of revenue	High Concentration in 1 Client
High Amount of Accounts Receivable	Low Amount of Accounts Receivable

There is not an exact formula for determining your percentage. You simply need to take into account all of the factors that cause risk. Some of these factors are outlined above. If your company tends to be leaning heavily toward one of the ends, then the number becomes apparent. If it is in the middle, then maybe 20% is your magic percentage. Again, this is not an exact science. If you want to err on the conservative side, lean towards 30%. Most of the factors can be seen above. Let's discuss a few of them.

Here's one of your biggest factors. If you have a lot of concentration in one or two clients, you have a higher risk factor. If one of those clients drops off, you suddenly have a bunch of employees getting paid by you, but you don't have a client to bill. If that's you, your goal is to have 30% of your annualized revenue. Take your annual revenue, multiply it by

30%, and that's your cash on hand. Or at least, it should be. Again, you can swallow now.

You're also a 30-percenter, by the way, if you constantly need to go out and find a lot of new clients every month. On the other hand, if you have a lot of recurring revenue built up in your business, then 10% is probably enough because you don't have as much risk.

Long-range plans can play a role. Maybe you're thinking about acquiring or even building a new building —you'll need cash for that. Perhaps you're reaching the point where a partner is going to be leaving in the next few years —you want to start building cash for that.

Matt Westgate:

> What we've been able to do with our cash reserve is make an investment in our people and a commitment to people in a way that we would otherwise be unable to. We can have someone that maybe isn't working on a project for a client, we can have them around for a month or two, and maybe they're helping us, more often than not, on some sort of internal project or exploring some R&D components. We're starting to see the benefits of that investment with some other products that we've created. We actually spun off a sister organization last year, called Drupalize.Me that does about a million in revenue. It's a whole different shift in our organization, but our Virtual CFO was the instigator of that. He was the one that said, "This is going to help your company. You may not understand

all the reasons why, but you need to do this in your organization."

If you're concerned your business is going to have a downturn, build up cash now. But don't build up too much. I think anything over 30% is overkill. Again, depending on your needs, some of that cash on hand shouldn't be on hand anymore, it should be paid out to the owner. Or used for a big purchase. Or bonuses to the staff, if you think that's appropriate.

So, let's go back to the questions I asked at the beginning of this chapter:

- How much cash do you have on hand?
- Do you know how much it should be?
- Now let me ask one last question: What are you going to do about it?

Chapter 2: Time is Money

"Time is an evil word. And really, it's kind of a lie. No matter what you put down it's never going to be 100% accurate." - Jody Grunden

What is an hour of your employees' time worth to you? You know what you're paying them per hour. You know what they're billing clients. But do you really know how well they're using their time? Are you getting your money's worth?

You know how many hours they work each week. Or at least, how many hours they say they work each week. No one is going to be 100% accurate on that, just as they aren't going to be 100% precise on how many hours they're billing for. They'll come close. So, you probably do a better job of tracking that than you think. And you should have a good handle on just how they're putting those hours in, how much time they're putting towards a project. But do you know how many hours they SHOULD be putting in? How much time should they be putting in, in order to achieve their goals? In other words, you probably know what they're doing, but you probably don't know what they *should* be doing.

That's one of the biggest things most business owners don't know, and it's one of the biggest problems we help our clients solve when we break it down for them. Let's get back to the forecast for a minute. When we break out time, you need to know what the end goal is. If you know what the end goal is, then you can back into the time breakdown. With your human capital, everything is going to be based on time in some way, whether you track it or not. But tracking it gives you a clear picture. It doesn't matter if you track it by the week, by the month, or even by the hour. It's still human capital and they can only work so much. Time is finite.

You have to decide how much time you want your team to bill toward client work each week. What's your weekly expectation? We have clients who want their team to bill as little as 30 hours a week, and then they're done. Others want 32, 34, 36, or more. We even have some clients who want their team to bill 40 hours per week towards client projects — meaning they are probably working in excess of 50 hours per week. Firms all have different expectations. That's built into the culture that they're trying to establish. It's important to understand what your end goal is going to be, and the culture you're trying to establish to fit that end goal.

So how often should you track time? Often. I recommend tracking time by the hour and recording it daily for each week. The reason we like to do it daily is not that we are horrible bosses, but because it fits our goals — going back to the forecasting model again. On average, with the digital marketing firms, we typically see firms with billable requirements between 32 and 34 hours per week.

Lori Gold Patterson:

> *One of the big things we learned is to take calculated risks. We always tracked over-budget hours. Hours that we had to do but that we didn't get paid for. We watched our trends and we had set where we should be*

and what we shouldn't go over. We actually thought any hours where you go over budget are bad. We thought we should be at zero, but we gave ourselves a little bit of play. What we learned with having a CFO is that we were too low. If you're too low, then you're not taking enough risks in what you're proposing and how you're proposing it. We learned to give ourselves the okay to understand that there should be a level of over-budget. Prior to that, we weren't in unison with the industry and their other clients. That's a gift that we gave to ourselves and to projects, to just be a little more risk-taking and be able to give a little bit more in situations with clients. That hasn't cost us more money. It's actually been a real benefit to our quality and our income. That was a new one for us.

I understand, nobody likes to keep track of time. Time is an evil word. And really, it's kind of a lie. No matter what you put down it's never going to be 100% accurate. There are a lot of people who are actually against tracking time for that reason. I completely disagree. I strongly believe that you have to track time in order to properly forecast revenue. Whether you are fixed fee, hourly billing, or even value billing, you still have to track it to figure out what your costs are so that you know how to properly price your service. The bottom line is when you track time you're just making sure that you're on target to hit your forecasted goals. And, your forecasted goals will result in profit — there is that word again.

If you don't have someone like me to help you do it, there are a lot of different time tracking tools out there that do a great job. Harvest, QuickBooks, FreshBooks, and 10,000 feet are just a few of the many different mechanisms to help you track time. You can even do it in Excel or Google Sheets if you want to. For the most part, it doesn't really make any difference which one you use. You just need to pick one that best fits your needs and do it. You need to be able to track it and then be able to allocate it to the clients, the jobs, and your team.

You don't need an accounting background. It's fairly simple once you understand what the end goal should be. For instance, when you track time, if you're looking at a regular employee who's going to work 40-hours per week for 52 weeks a year, that's 2,080 hours a year. Then you start subtracting vacation time, holidays, company retreats, and any other time that they will not be available to bill towards a client. We typically call this time "culture hours." Culture hours vary dramatically from firm to firm. The time that you have left after you remove your culture hours is your time available to work. Again, this number varies dramatically from firm to firm.

Your magic number could be 1,500 hours, it could be 1,600 hours, or it could be 1,700 hours. Don't get too hung up on what the number should be. The exact number is not important at this point. The important thing is that you know what that number is so that you can forecast properly. Then from there, you must take into account your company's weekly billing expectation. How many hours per week do you expect your team to bill each week? Take your weekly expectation multiplied by your available time to work and you come up with your expected billing hours per team member.

It could be any number of hours per year. Let's say it is 1,400 hours a year that they're going to bill out per producer. You now have a starting base on what each team member can produce in hours for your firm. Once you have determined the hours you can convert hours to dollars. It's pretty simple if you break it down.

Once we have the times built, then we look at the rates. Once you've determined how many billable hours you expect everyone on the team to work, then you have to break it down and look to see what they're actually billing toward a client. The first thing we look at is the average bill rate. What's the average rate that you bill toward a client? Not your standard rate. Not the rate that you quote a client. The rate that you actually earn — $200 per hour, $175 per hour? To calculate it, you simply take your revenue and divide it by the number of billable hours actually billed toward the project. Remember, your average bill rate is the true measure of what you're getting.

Now we have all of the components to properly forecast. Because if you know how much that individual should be able to generate and you know how much that individual costs, you should be able to calculate the gross profit that individual can bring to the company.

It all comes back to forecasting and this is a huge tool for that. Once we know the average bill rate and the utilization rate, you multiply the two together and that's your effective rate. Your all-in rate. That's the rate you really can't mess around with. That's the rate you can actually manage or monitor all the way through the process of forecasting, to determine if your forecasting is accurate, if you're on track or not, and the different levers you need to pull if you aren't on track.

In addition to being able to forecast better, it will also help you to become more efficient. Tracking employees' time can sometimes help you streamline your processes. Once you've put your forecast together, identified all your key performance indicators and learned how to manage them, you should be able to effectively make course corrections when things in the business are not going as planned. You may end up digging deeper into why your average bill rate is nowhere near your standard rate. Or, you might find out why, although you are planning on a 60 percent utilization rate, you consistently fall short by 10 percent. When looking into the utilization rates for individuals on the team you may notice that some are not meeting expectations. You can then address the situation. It's not that you're picking on a certain individual, you are trying to identify a problem to fix. You may find that every time a person does this type of job, they fall down or they don't meet expectations. You may be able to get that person trained in that area.

Or if things aren't going well overall on that job, maybe a different type of billing is in order. Maybe you find out that all of your flat fee billing jobs are significantly missing the target. Maybe it helps you to determine that you are quoting it wrong. Or maybe you need to add an extra 10-15% every time you quote a flat fee job because you now know that you inherently underestimate. There are levers you can pull. You might find you're doing everything right but you're still not hitting the bottom line number you need to hit. That's when you look at increasing your prices, or making a personnel change and bringing in someone at a lower level to get that job done at a lower cost.

We help our clients track time, but we do it ourselves too, and that has helped us. We do some digging and find out, "Hey, this job is taking three hours to do and we really can only invoice a client for two hours. We need to figure out how we can streamline the process in order to get it within budget." It might mean introducing new technology. We might uncover, with a little research, some technology that may save two hours on that job and get us closer to our budgeted number. Or, even better, hit our targeted number. It's important to analyze the information that you've got so you can actually make informed decisions. Informed decisions are obviously key to running a successful business.

Anytime you can streamline the process and do things more efficiently then, obviously, the bottom line is going to be bigger than if you're doing things all over the place and in a chaotic way. It's so important to take a look and analyze this on a regular weekly or monthly basis. Don't wait until the end of the year to figure out what you did wrong. Use this as a tool to manage your company, not as a whip but as a way to educate your team. You can educate yourself as well and find different ways of making things more effective and more efficient.

When we talk this through with new clients we can start to see the "light bulb turning on inside their head." And while that light bulb is shining brightly they can start to see the path to their future a lot clearer. When you break it down completely and analyze it all the way down to the bottom line profit number, it's really an eye-opener for them. When we talk about forecasting, they always ask, "How would you even know how much money you're going to make?" It would be cool if everything ended at the planning stages, but obviously, it doesn't. You need to know what your team is set up to do, and then you have to go out and get the work.

The first thing is, based on the people you have, when you break it down completely, you need to know how much money you should be generating each month. Then you need to know why that amount is different month to month — even though you have the same number of people the number of days each month varies as well as vacation days. You also need to factor in retreats or other things that would affect your expectations. Really, it just comes down to basic math, but it's a complete eye-opener for people. It's an "aha!" moment when we break it out for them. They might be able to figure out their utilization rate and other things, but they often don't understand why they're figuring it out.

What we do is look at what they currently have and what their real expectations should be. Based on that, we can model their whole year out and figure out exactly what kind of profit level it is and what kind of cash they should be generating. Often, they find out that their margin between what they charge a client and what their team member charges them is significantly lower than what it needs to be. What now? They have to figure a way to make that margin or gap bigger. As a result, we'll often advise them to increase their prices. Or, their price may be right where it should be but their average billing rate is a lot lower. Or, maybe a lower dollar team member should be performing the work that a senior team member is doing. Again, why does it happen in the first place? It could happen because when they do their quotes they underestimate the time it takes, or maybe the team is just inefficient and takes too much time, or maybe they don't even know how much time they're supposed to be taking — they get the job done but they're always over.

You can also determine if you're understaffed or overstaffed. For example, if your utilization rate is expected to be 60% and it's constantly at 50%, that means you're overstaffed. It's pretty simple.   You need to cut back in certain areas. On the other hand, if your expected rate is 60% and you're always hitting 65 to 70%, that means you might be pushing it a little bit and maybe you're one or two people shy of what you need. That's when you go back to the model, put an extra person in there and see how that impacts the bottom line and the overall culture of the company. These are all things where you can actually make a real change which will have a real impact. Changing personnel, changing the type of billing, and changing the type of work all come into the analysis as you properly monitor time.

Maybe this happens to you: Every time you do a design work you're always over and you never meet budget. Well, there are some issues there. A lot of the time it comes right down to pricing, expectation, quoting — all the different things on the outside that are now conveyed down to the people.

Have you heard the term "scope creep"? It's a profit killer. Let's say you've got a job and the billing gets quoted at

$1,000. You budgeted 10 hours at $100 an hour. You get nine hours into the job and the client wants this little extra change made. Instead of stopping at 10 hours, or actually billing for the change, you just throw it in because you think, "we can do it quickly, no big deal." But all of a sudden, you're up to 15 hours, you're over budget, and it's too late to go back and bill the client because it was never agreed upon in the first place.

That's where the expectations are so important. When you're billing time, it's important for the team to know what all the expectations are and what's involved in them. You have to be informative when you're doing your project management. You have to clearly explain to the team what their job is and what the scope is so you don't have that scope creep. It's really easy to happen, especially if it's one of the owners that's actually working on the job because they tend to give a lot away, whereas the team members really don't have that privilege and can give less away.

As you can see, tracking time is a valuable practice that you need to be sure you are utilizing.

Chapter 3: Productivity = Profitability

"You have to take the emotion out of everything. You have to look at what kind of production each person can do. " - Jody Grunden

We know you've been tracking your employees' time, but tracking time is just an element of tracking productivity. There has to be a purpose to time tracking otherwise, there's no reason to do it. For us, the main purpose of tracking time is to determine the capacity of each of our team members so we can build a strong forecast.

Productivity is a function of time. Productivity, as defined by Investopedia is "an economic measure of output per unit of input."[2] Input would be defined as labor dollars while output would be defined as revenue dollars. It is important that we look at both revenue and expense. Too often we find business owners chasing revenue dollars and not spending enough time controlling labor dollars. This is a big mistake!

Let's look at the labor dollars first. When we look at productivity, we're looking at the total amount that we're actually paying a person. That is pretty simple. We just need to know the production team's total salary, right? Wrong. Salary is just the starting point. We need to take into consideration all of the hard costs associated with the employee in addition to the salary. These costs are called burden. Some of the direct burden costs would include 401(k), profit sharing plans, health insurance, life insurance,

---

[2] http://www.investopedia.com/terms/p/productivity.asp

disability insurance, technology stipends, education stipends, and, of course, we cannot forget the employer portion of payroll taxes. Once we have identified all of the burden costs, we will add burden to the production team's salary. Now we have identified the total cost of our production team.

If you would like to know what your burden rate is you would simply divide the total burden cost by the total salary [Burden/Salary]. We typically see burden rates in the area of 20 to 25%. So now that we know what our total production costs are we can determine what the revenue should be. Simple math would say to multiply total production cost by two and that number should roughly be your team's revenue, but it is a little more complicated than that.

The complication starts with how you bill the client. There are several different ways to bill clients — hourly, flat fee, value-based, sprint based, and recurring revenue are just a few. And to make it even more complicated, many firms may use some of the above, all of the above, and/or a hybrid of the above. Let's take a quick look at each.

Hourly Billing

Hourly billing is just what it sounds like, billing a client by the amount of time that they work on a project. There are several ways to determine the dollar rate at which they bill. First of all, we call this rate the standard rate. The company can base the standard rate on internal costs. For instance, they can create the rate by using a multiple of cost — 3 to 4 times cost is a popular method. They can also create the rate on what the market is bearing — what is everyone else charging? No matter how they come up with the standard rate, the gist of hourly billing is standard rate multiplied by time.

I have never completely understood why companies would bill by the hour. Ultimately billing by the hour pits the company against their client. It also rewards the company for inefficiencies. That being said, let's discuss the model and allow you to make the decision.

As I had mentioned earlier, the hourly billing model charges the client an hourly rate for everything you do. The rate can be based upon a single rate (commonly referred to as a blended rate) taking into account the collective experience of the individuals that will be working on the project. Or, there can be multiple rates for multiple individuals on the project. Maybe an architect would command a $300 per hour rate, while a junior developer might only get a rate of $125 per hour.

The rate doesn't always have to be based on the individual, it can also be based on the type of work being performed. Work that has a low perceived value may be billed at a lower rate while work that has a high perceived value may be billed at a higher rate.

The nice thing about hourly billing is that it puts the risk on the client. What do I mean by that? If you underestimated the project and run over on hours, you simply bill the client for the actual number of hours worked. So, in theory, you get paid for every hour worked.

Not too fast. Clients often push back when the number of hours billed is greater than the number of hours estimated. Immediately, you are in an adversarial relationship with your client. Everything that you do from then on gets put under a microscope. Should that task have taken 3 hours or should it have taken only 1.5 hours?

Not only can the number of hours be scrutinized, but also the person working the project. Should a senior member of the team have handled that task or should it have been handled by a junior member?

It can also penalize your team for being efficient with their time. The more efficient that your team works, the lesser you get paid for that work. Something about that just doesn't seem right.

Flat-Fee Billing

Flat-fee billing comes with many names — milestone pricing, sprint billing, fixed-scope pricing and fixed bid pricing are just a few of the names that are commonly used. All of these things have one thing in common — the bill is based on time but does not fluctuate with time. We can safely say that flat-fee billing is simply a variation of hourly billing. The company estimates how many hours it will take to complete a project. They multiply the number of hours by their standard rate. Sound familiar? They may give themselves a buffer by adding 10% or so to the price, but once they have the price, the price becomes fixed. So, as you can guess, any overages on time will kill a flat-fee project. The estimation of time on the front end and the execution of time during the project is essential.

The nice thing about flat fee billing is that it creates predictability. Predictability for both the client and the company. There is no guessing game on how much a project is going to cost. Everything is agreed upon upfront — kind of a novel idea. No different than buying a cup of coffee or a stick of gum.

As it should, flat-fee billing puts the risk squarely on the shoulders of the company. It rewards the company for becoming efficient with their work. The more efficient a company is, the higher their profitability potential. Flat-fee billing forces a company to look for and seek out efficiencies within their team.

If using a flat-fee pricing model, it is important that the project manager understands how the job was priced. The profitability of the project now rests on her shoulders. Why on her shoulders? Because we all know that as soon as the job starts, everything starts to change. Is this new request from the client part of the original agreement or is it outside of the scope of the agreement? If it is outside the scope of the agreement, how do you get compensated for the change? If not done immediately, then the inaction could lead to an adversarial relationship — again, not good.

A nice side effect of flat-fee billing is that it creates a few long-term benefits. The two biggest benefits are developed processes and empowered people. It forces the company to develop processes for all types of tasks. Processes lead to efficiencies. It also forces the company to leverage its team members. The more work that can be pushed down to junior team members, the more profitable the job. Developing processes and leveraging people equals profitability.

Retainer-Based Billing

Retainer-based billing is very common in the digital marketing industry. This type of billing is based on hours, but the company will tell the client that they are going to allot a set amount of hours per week on their project. The company presents the client with the cost based on the number of hours agreed upon and a set hourly rate. The client can have access to a specific person or a team for the agreed upon amount of hours each week. With retainer-based billing, if the client doesn't use the time, they lose it. If they use more than the agreed upon number of hours, they're billed an additional amount at the end of the month to compensate for that difference.

When digital marketing companies use the "retainer-based billing" method, it's different than what an attorney calls a "retainer." When an attorney bills a "retainer," they get money up front. It's an advance. As soon as they work through the money they've received, then they request more money and the billing gets applied every period towards that retainer and the attorney will ask for additional money to apply toward future billings. If there's anything leftover at the end, then the attorney is technically supposed to send that back to the client. This differs completely from how a "retainer" is used in the digital marketing world where if it's not used it's gone because they're basically making that person available as opposed to eating up the time, but if the person does use more time, then it's compensated for.

Value-Based Billing

Value-based billing, or value billing, is a completely different monster. Value billing has a variety of meanings and is used in a variety of different ways. The difference between value billing and the other two billing methods we just covered is that it is not based upon hours. It can be looked at as a percentage of the overall return on the value that a client receives from the service.

This can be hard to determine and could require the customer to open up their books to the company. "Value" could be the value of a service or a "person" replaced. It could be the value put on a specific deliverable, such as creating a logo or painting a picture. It could be a flat fee with values placed on different types of service irrespective of the hours that it takes to perform the service.

The best way for me to explain value billing is by looking at the NFL. Yep, the National Football League. Let's look at a 53-man roster and see what type of value each position yields. Then let's pretend that each position is a different company. Here are some of the assumptions that I am going to make:

- Each player graduated from college, so they are smart.

- Each player puts a ton of time in the gym, so they are athletic.
- Each player goes to each of the practices, so they are hard working.
- Each player watches a ton of game film, so they are prepared.

Based on the above assumptions you would think that each player gets paid the same amount, but that is wrong. Did you know that the average quarterback charges $4 million to play in the league while the average football player across all positions charges $1.9 million? And, oh, by the way, Andrew Luck of the Indianapolis Colts commands a salary of $24 million.

Why can Luck charge more for his service than the average football player? Is it based on the number of hours he prepares for the game? Not really. It can be argued that Luck possesses a unique skill that many teams value. That value is in no way based on hours, so he is able to command a value-based salary limited to only what the market can bear.

Value-based billing is near and dear to my heart because this is how we have been billing our clients for the last 3 to 4 years. Prior to that, we attempted to bill our clients on a fixed fee basis that was based strictly on time. We found out that we were horrible estimators of time. What a mistake for us — it almost put us out of business! We realized after failing miserably for 10 years that it was almost impossible to accurately estimate a flat fee for our line of work. Every client is different, no matter how we tried to rationalize them as being the same. Also, we were, in effect, competing with all of the other accounting firms who were billing hourly — yuck.

Then we made the dramatic shift to value billing. We began billing at what the market would and could bear to replace our bundled service package internally, then discounted it down to what we believed the market could bear. Should CFO work be billed out at a higher dollar amount than bookkeeping? Absolutely. Our fixed-bid system did not allow for that because it was based on time. We had to determine what was more valuable to a client. As we went through all of our processes, putting a value on each, we started making changes to our billing structure to better match value with price. No longer are we basing our price on time as we did so many years ago with fixed-fee billing. We now base our prices on value. With that, I am sure we will have to continue to make changes along the way as our perceived value goes up and down.

In order to value bill, you have to determine the services that the customer values the most and price accordingly. You also have to do the inverse for services that the customer does not value as much. Once you have determined those two things, you then have to determine how much the market can bear for the service. The last thing you have to do is make an educated guess on how much each of the services will cost to make sure it is worth offering those services in the first place.

When companies value bill, it doesn't mean they are charging the client the most. It just means that the company is basing their pricing on value instead of time.

A perfect example of this happened to me a few years ago. I was outside playing catch with my son when he let the ball get away from him and it hit the house, hitting the only window in the area. Crash! I called the window repair company, and I told them what happened. They said they would send a person out the next day and it would cost $750 to fix the window (value bill). I thought that was a great deal because I definitely did not possess the skills to do the work myself. The serviceman came out the next day and replaced the window in about 15 minutes. I knew the price in advance and was happy to hand him a check for $750. Win-win for everyone. Doing some quick math, if the material cost $250 and he only spent 15 minutes to fix the window, he effectively made $2,000 per hour — hmmm. I am pretty confident if he told me that he was going to charge $2,000 per hour, I would have called another window repairman.

Circling back to my company, it took a lot of confidence in our team and in our quoting ability to value bill properly. It took a ton of trial and error. We discovered the hard way that finding out what the market values for your service is really hard. Most of the time, as owners, we are either too hard on ourselves and undervalue our service or overconfident in ourselves and overvalue our service. I find that if we have a 35% or more successful closing ratio, then we are priced about right. Too high of a closing ratio generally means that we are undervaluing our service, while the converse means that we are overvaluing our service.

In all, value billing is a unique pricing strategy that is based on the value delivered to the customer. It is not based on time, cost, margin, or historical prices.

Enough said. Now let's compare the three types of billing. Here's a perfect example of the difference between the three billing methods loosely based on one my favorite movies, *The Accountant*. It's an awesome title, awesome movie, and an awesome career — just saying.

In the movie, the main character is a CPA who is hired by a company that is about to go public to solve a mystery that they believe to be employee embezzlement. The Accountant is asked to analyze the last 12 years' worth of data. For reference, an employee of the company spent over a month analyzing one year's worth of data and could not find anything. Twelve hours later the Accountant not only determined conclusively that a form of embezzlement had occurred but also the exact amount of money that was embezzled— well in the millions of dollars — and by whom. Not bad for a day's worth of work...or was it?

Let's look that the different types of billings. Keep in mind that the Accountant was extremely smart and sought after. He would easily command an hourly billing rate of at least $300 per hour. For this example, let's go with a billing rate of $300 per hour. As I mentioned, no matter how many hours he would have estimated beforehand that it would take to complete the job, the job took 12 hours to complete. So, simple math would tell you that he would have billed the client for his 12 hours of work for a total of $3,600 (12 hours x $300). That's a very profitable day.

Now, let's say the Accountant decided to bill on a flat fee. He might rationalize the billing this way: He noticed that it took an employee one month to analyze one year. He is smarter and could do it quicker than that employee. Plus, he is pretty confident that the employee was doing other things and could no way have been devoting 100% of her time to the project. With all of that rationalized, he is estimating that it will take 3 months at 40 hours per week to complete the project. How would he have determined the bill? He would have broken the months down to hours. Doing so, he would have calculated his fee to be $156,000 (520 hours x $300).That's much better. But he probably would have looked at that dollar amount and discounted it further just to get the deal. Sound familiar? He probably would have determined the fee to be $149,000.

Finally, let's say that the Accountant decides to value bill. First of all, he is extremely confident that he can deliver. He knows that he is in high demand. He has a unique skill. He also knows that if he does not deliver, it could potentially stall the process of the company going public. So, based on that, he tries to determine a value that the client would pay to achieve the result agreed upon. He presents a price up front to the client in the amount of $250,000 to solve the mystery.

Which billing method did the Accountant use? You guessed it. He value-billed the client. The client thought the price was reasonable and agreed to the deal up front. Now break down *that* hourly rate — wow!

It worked out this time around, but it doesn't always happen that way. What if he couldn't solve the mystery? He'd get nothing. What if it took him years to solve the mystery? That could have resulted in him working for pennies on the dollar. He definitely made the right choice this time because he was confident that he could deliver on the value the customer wanted.

Now that we have determined which type of billing you will be doing, we need to make sure that you properly recognize revenue. Should revenue be recognized on a Cash basis, Tax basis, Accrual basis or some other type of method? Before we decide on which is the correct method, let's look at each one.

Cash Basis

Cash basis accounting is pretty much what it sounds like. You recognize revenue when you receive the money and recognize expenses when you pay the money. Pretty simple, right? Wrong. What do you do if the client pays you a big sum of money at the onset of the engagement and you haven't worked an hour? One month (when you received the money) could look strong, followed by the next month (when you paid the employees) that looks weak. Although often I would advise using this method to pay taxes, I would not recommend using this method to determine profitability. The timing of payments is so crucial using this method that it really doesn't make sense to determine profitability with it.

Tax Basis

Tax basis accounting is similar to cash basis. The only difference is the adjustments you make to correspond with tax laws. Do you depreciate assets based on tax law at the time of the purchase or base the depreciation on the accrual method of accounting? Banks hate the tax basis method because it looks to them like they have no collateral to lend against because you expensed all equipment purchases in the year that you bought them. Using this option for financial statement reporting limits a ton of lending opportunities. I could bore you with many more examples, but let's move on.

Accrual Basis

The accrual basis is the method that I recommend. What the accrual method does is it matches revenue when the money is earned and expenses when they occur. It has nothing to do with when you create a bill for a vendor or create an invoice for a client. It has everything to do with recognizing revenue when your team worked on the project and the corresponding costs associated with that project in the same period. It is very important to match your revenue and expenses to get a complete understanding of your company and project profitability. If there is a mismatch, the forecast could be completely misleading. Now, you may be thinking, "if I report financials on an accrual basis does that mean that I have to prepare my taxes on an accrual basis?" The answer is no. Your tax advisor should simply be able to convert your financial statements from an accrual basis to a cash basis at tax time.

Now that we have identified the two main elements of your gross profit (revenue recognition and production expense), simply subtracting the production expense from the revenue determines your gross profit. In Chapter 4 we will determine how to predict your revenue if you use hourly billing or flat-fee billing. For those of us who use value billing, we will touch on how to predict revenue there as well —we added a half a chapter (Chapter 4.5) to cover that topic.

Chapter 4: The Levers You Can Pull – The Production Metrics

"Even the smallest of changes can have a huge impact on your bottom line." - Jody Grunden

You're used to pulling levers. You do it in a voting booth. You do it at a slot machine. In both cases, you hope you're lucky with the results. But what about your business? What if there were a bunch of levers you could pull that could also pay off for you and improve your company's performance? Actually, there are. Our clients use them all the time. And unlike that slot machine, it isn't about luck. These levers have a guaranteed payoff.

Before we tell you what they are and how you can use them, we need to give you a little Accounting 101. The levers are what we, in the accounting world, call "Key Performance Indicators." The key word there is <u>Indicators</u>. A Key Performance Indicator (KPI) is a gauge that a business can use to determine how successful they are at any given point in time, and that can be both financial and non-financial. KPIs are things the owner of the business can control and use to affect how profitable the business is. The levers that we are going to pull in this chapter pertain to hourly billing and fixed-fee billing. Value billing is a beast by itself and will be addressed later. No matter which type of billing you use, it is important to understand how these levers could impact your company.

Lever number one is Utilization. That's the amount of time actually billed to clients compared to the time that is available to work. For example, if you're looking at one specific employee, you're looking at the amount that one person will bill towards client projects over a period of a year compared with the time that person has available to work during the year, not taking into account vacation time, sick days, educational time or any other non-billable time. All of these things impact what the utilization rate should be, but when it comes down to it the utilization rate is the number of hours billed divided by the number of working hours available to bill. So, how do you change the utilization rate? You add or remove some of those variables. You make available either more or less time an employee can work on client projects. Then you make sure that they have the client projects to work on. More time can be better. But depending on the pay rate and skill sets, you might want to give certain employees less time for client work and more time for administrative duties.

Lever number two is Weekly Expectation. This is also part of the utilization. Weekly expectation is what we expect a particular employee to bill during a particular week. That's assuming it's a normal work week — they aren't on vacation, they don't have continuing education, there isn't a holiday, nothing like that. Let's say that person works a 40-hour work week on a regular weekly basis. If they have 40 hours to work, how many hours do you want them to bill — 30? 32? 35? The most common range is somewhere between 32 and 34 hours per week. Keep in mind that although you pay them for 40 hours a week, part of their time goes towards administrative and other non-billable tasks.

UTILIZATION			
Total Working Hours	2,080		
Less Company Culture	- 408	Total Billable Hours	1,254
Total Available Hours	1,672	Total Working Hours	/ 2,080
Weekly Expectation	x 75%	**UTILIZATION**	**60.29%**
Total Billable Hours	**1,254**		

Lever number three is Standard Bill Rates. That's the amount you actually price the project. There are a lot of different ways to price projects and every company is a little different in this regard. Say you go by hourly rate, and you're going to price the project at $175 per hour, assuming it's an hourly project. There's your standard bill rate. That's what's in your quote, or your signed agreement with the client. You both agree on what the client will pay. It doesn't have to be an hourly rate. It can be a flat fee. That's how we charge our clients. It can be a flat fee per day, per week, per month, or an overall lump sum flat fee. It's simple multiplication: hourly rate times the number of hours you expect the project to take. And hopefully you're right about the number of hours. If you estimate wrong, you're basically back to that slot machine lever.

Lever number four is the Average Bill Rate. How is that different than the standard bill rate? The average bill rate is what actually happened. Instead of multiplying, we divide. We look back at the sales price and divide that by the number of billable hours actually worked. You'd be surprised how many times it comes out to a completely different number —

sometimes higher, sometimes lower. It depends on how much of a write-up or write-down the projects have. Sometimes there are over-runs. You end up working more than what you had in the quote, but you can't bill for it. Now your average bill rate is lower. We don't like that. If you get the job done quicker than what you actually billed for and you can still bill the standard rate, your average bill rate is going to be higher. We like that. It might be equal to the standard rate, which is fine too. It all comes down to how much it actually takes to work on the project versus what was quoted. Have you been accurate in this area? Do you know?

Standard Rate	180
Write-down	(16)
AVERAGE BILLABLE RATE	**164**

Lever number five is Increasing or Decreasing FTE's. An FTE is a full-time equivalent employee. That's not every employee. In this case, we're talking about producers. We're talking about those employees who do work that's directly billed to clients. Obviously, you also have administrative people, and how many of those you have affects your bottom line, but that's a one-to-one ratio. If you add a $35,000 administrative person, you subtract $35,000 from your profits. But the lever you can pull that has the greatest impact is producers. They generate revenue. So, we look at how many you have, what you're paying them, and how much revenue they're producing. This helps answer a very important question: Do you have the right number of them? Does it make sense to add an FTE? How much increased revenue and increased profit will result from that increased investment in salary? On the flip side, when many companies pull this lever, it reveals the need to reduce their staff. Either way, it answers their question.

Using the Utilization and Standard rate metrics, the following breakdown is the calculation used to determine what each producer in your company should generate in revenue. Assuming 17 FTE producers, you can calculate the revenue that your team is built to produce. Plug in your own numbers and see how far off you are.

Total Hours	2,080
Less: Culture Hours	408
Available Hours	1,672
Hours Per Week	30
Divided by: Total Available Weekly Hours	40
Weekly Expecation	75%
Available Hours	1,672
Times: Weekly Expectation	75%
Total Billable Hours	1,254
Total Billable Hours	1,254
Divided by: Total Hours	2,080
Utilization Rate	60%
Standard Rate	180
Less: Write Downs (9% in this case)	(16)
Average Bill Rate	164
Total Billable Hours	1,254
Times: Average Bill Rate	164
Total Revenue Per FTE	205,656
Total Revenue Per FTE	205,656
Times: Total FTEs	17
Total Estimated Revenue	**3,496,152**

The first four levers: Utilization, Weekly Expectation, Standard Bill Rate and Average Bill Rate all lead to your Effective Rate. That's your "all-in." Basically, that means taking the number of billable hours you can actually bill to a client and dividing it into the number of hours you actually pay the employee. Another way to look at is the Utilization rate times the Average Bill Rate. We call that the "no cheat rate." It is what it is. There's no lying about hours, no manipulating the numbers. Employees can't fluctuate how they record their time versus administrative or billable work. The effective rate is what really matters, and it's the easiest rate to track once you know how to define the other four.

So, you might be wondering, why wouldn't increasing or decreasing FTE's also affect the Effective Rate? Technically they do because the other four are based on one full-time equivalent employee. That's assuming they're being utilized properly, and checking these numbers will help you verify that. Adding an FTE will impact the other levers if you bring one on without having the sales to support that addition. Then the overall company Effective Rate will go down, which is something we try to avoid.

The benefit to pulling these levers is twofold — it helps you now and it helps you in the future. We tell our clients to monitor these numbers very carefully, whether it's on a weekly basis, monthly basis, or however often they choose. If they watch all of these, then they know where they're at. And, they're able to change where they will be in the future. The benefit is not just keeping your bottom line better now, it adjusts your billing going forward and your forecasting.

Here's something else to think about. You don't have to pull the lever completely down. You can make adjustments with little things. For example, you can look to see how one hour of extra billing per week will impact the bottom line. Not working? What about two hours? Maybe you're still not where you need to be, so how else can you impact this? Maybe you look at your standard rate and decide you can probably bill $10 or $20 more per hour. Where does that get you? Then you can look at the average bill rate and maybe you find out your people aren't producing at that rate and there is a huge write-down. What can you do to improve your people process so they're billing closer to that standard rate? Maybe you need to educate them a little more or show them a different process, how to do something a little bit more efficiently. You can pull one lever all the way or you can pull some of the levers just a little bit and tweak them a little bit at a time. This is why it's so important to understand all of these levers and how they all work together.

The impact of the different levers can be dramatic. Even the smallest of changes can have a huge impact on your bottom line. It could be in the hundreds of thousands of dollars in many cases, depending on how many full-time equivalents you have. Just changing any one of these can have a significant impact on the bottom line. And the combination can really be significant. Think of it like compounding interest — one lever will do a certain amount, two levers won't just double that amount, it could triple it, or quadruple it, or more.

Here are some hard numbers: Two levers can have an impact of $150,000 to $300,000 on a 15-producer company.

Remember that 10% to 30% cash reserve we mentioned earlier? If you're having trouble getting there, pulling these levers can show you dramatically how you can actually get there pretty quickly just by making some internal changes.

This changes the way people think. When people aren't hitting their margin, the first thing a lot of business owners do is look at reducing marketing or administrative costs. In reality, they should look at their production people and look how they can make them more effective and more efficient or develop better processes where they can do their jobs easier and a lot better. Or maybe it's just the quoting that's wrong. What's everybody else charging an hour? Are we that much different? Are we $30 or $40 different? Maybe that's why we're getting all the jobs that are putting us out of business. That's the power of understanding how the math works inside the company.

When we show this to a client, the impact is amazing. The client's eyes get really big. They look at it and they're just astounded. The first time I presented this to an owner the dollar amount came out to about $300,000 just by a $10 increase in their standard price. You should have seen their jaws hit the floor. Often business owners just don't realize the huge significance of a small action.

What I've shown you in this chapter is in many ways just the tip of the iceberg when it comes to these levers. There's too much information to cover in just one chapter. I'll go into more detail on levers in Chapters 7 and 8. Could this be any more exciting?

Seriously, this is exciting stuff. Have you pulled any of these levers in your business? Do you know the feeling you get when that slot machine comes up with three 7's? It's the same kind of feeling you get when you see this type of impact on your bottom line, with one distinct difference — you can control it.

Chapter 4.5: Predicting Revenue with Value Billing

"Create more value than you capture." – Tim O' Reilly

Again, I want to stress that value billing does not take into account hours and profit margins. Value billing is based on the perceived value for the service rendered. Because there is not a correlation between hours and price, not all of the levers in Chapter 4 will work. Instead, you will want to focus on a few other metrics in determining revenue. I will get to that in a few minutes.

First, how do you define Value Billing? That is a good question because there are many different ways of looking at it. Often the approaches are at extreme ends.

One approach is to base your price on the determined end value that the client will receive from your service. For instance, if you are working on a project for a client and they believe that because of your work they will generate $1 million in additional revenue or reduce their costs by that same amount, you could offer to charge a percentage of the projected revenue generated or projected cost savings. If you believe that 10 percent seems to be a fair rate, you could charge the client $100K for the project. The challenge when using this method is that often it is too hard to determine the true benefit received. And if the benefit is known, often the project manager may be unwilling to share that information or, because of internal policy, cannot share that information.

Entrepreneur and author, Tim O'Reilly defines value with a simple statement, "Create More Value Than You Capture."[3] Let's analyze that statement. Is he saying to share a direct portion of the value created? No. Is he saying that value is determined on an internal gross profit margin? No. He is simply saying that you should charge less than the value of what you are creating.

Based on O'Reilly's definition of value, what's next? Do we price our valuable service at a dollar? Do we go to the other extreme and price our valuable service at an amount of the project value less a dollar? Of course, neither of these approaches would be reasonable. This gives you a pretty large range to price your product. So, you have to determine what the market will bear.

The easiest way for me to do this is to relate back to my company and our services. We are a CPA firm that specializes in Virtual CFO Services. When I say "specialize in," I mean it. Ninety percent of what our firm does is to provide Virtual CFO Services for clients throughout the United States. How would we price our services? We know from experience that we provide a ton of value for our clients. Our clients generally show higher profit margins, an increase in working capital, and a sense of relief that a qualified person or business is overseeing their company.

So, how do we price our service? Let's take a quick look under our hood for some insight on how we came up with our

---

[3] http://ecorner-legacy.stanford.edu/podcasts/3054/Create-More-Value-Than-You-Capture

pricing model. We first wanted to determine what costs we were replacing. Because we bundle our service, we often replace the existing tax accountant and bookkeeper. Then we look at what a typical CFO would cost. In most areas of the nation, a qualified CFO would cost somewhere north of $125K in salary, plus about 25 percent in burden costs. All in, a company would pay somewhere around $150K to bring a qualified CFO onto their team. A tax accountant would cost around $10K for business and personal taxes, tax planning, and quarterly tax projections. A bookkeeper on staff would cost somewhere around $35K plus about 20% in burden. All in, a bookkeeper would cost around $42K. So, when we add them up, we get a total cost of approximately $200K. Wow, that is a ton of money. And, it could be even more if you live in New York City, San Diego, San Francisco, or any other large city across the US.

Now you are probably thinking, "if I could afford $200K on 'Accounting', I would not be thinking about bringing a Virtual CFO on board." True. Realizing that, maybe half of a CFO would work. Half of a CFO? Wouldn't it be nice to buy a half or even a quarter of a person? That being said, we know that a typical client is willing to pay between $50K to $100K for our services depending on where they are in their internal growth cycle. How do we know that? Well, we didn't know that until we tested the market. When we rolled out our service, we found that we typically close between 35 to 45% of the proposals that we submit.

Now that we have the price a prospect will pay for our valuable service, we have to determine if the service would be profitable at that rate. So, here is where we start crunching some internal numbers. Can we put together a team of accountants (typically 4 to 5 accountants performing different roles) to work part-time on a client and still make a reasonable profit? We have determined that we can more times than not if the team properly leverages one another.

The magic behind value billing is that you know how much you are going to charge before you start working on the engagement. Another note is that our engagements are perpetual, meaning it goes on forever until one of the parties terminates it. Not all value bill engagements are designed that way. Some have a defined start and stop. Either way, because the price is known, we should be able to take advantage of this.

Here is where we introduce you to the **subscription-based model**. The subscription-based model is taking over the software industry and is creeping into other industries. The basic theme is that you pay a perpetual recurring fee for a service. The fee is generally a fixed fee; therefore, it does not change month to month or week to week. Often the fee is automatically charged to a credit card or even better debited directly from the client's bank account. The huge benefit that the subscription-based model provides is that you no longer have to be in the banking industry for your clients. The subscription-based model practically eliminates all accounts receivable. Imagine what it would be like not having to chase down money that is owed to you.

So how does that pertain to your company? Well, it's pretty simple. If you know how much you are going to charge a client annually, why not break the payment down into 12-month payments? Better yet, why don't you break down the payment into 52 weekly payments? For instance, if the fee is determined to be $78K a year, the weekly payment would be $1,500 per week.

How do we properly forecast when we use Value-Based Billing? The two key metrics that we look at are average price and frequency of the sale. Average price is pretty simple. Frequency of the sale is a little tougher. Often, you have to rely on historical information. Or, if you are beginning this process, you have to rely on needed revenue based on your forecast. Then, adjust the number as you start to develop history. For instance, we know from historical data that our average client is roughly $1,100 per week. We also know that our demand over the past three years has been, on average, 2 to 3 new clients per month. So, if our current base of weekly clients is $80,000 and we know from that our frequency is expected to be $2K to $3K of additional weekly revenue each month, you can see how it is relatively easy to forecast revenue.

Don't forget to take churn into account because no matter how great your service is, clients will eventually leave for various reasons — good and bad. With our practice, we expect that we will lose approximately 3 to 5 percent of our clients per year. That has held true for quite some time. The most common reason we have found that a client leaves is actually a really good reason — the client builds the business up to a point where we help them sell. Leaving our firm in that manner is probably one of the most rewarding things that a client could ever do. So, when I am referring to adding 2 to 3 new clients per month, I am talking about net new clients per month.

Now that we have built a solid on-going revenue stream through value billing, what should our gross profit be? That gets a little more complex and somewhat subjective. The reason for that goes back to the idea that the quote was not based on time, but the metrics discussed earlier *were* based upon time. So, now what?

Here is where you have to determine your team's **capacity.** I am not sure that there is a mathematical way to determine this for three reasons: Clients, Team members, and Tasks.

Clients. You have to love them or, in some cases, hate them. What do I mean by that? With value-based billing, you are going to win on some clients and you are going to lose on some clients. Winning and losing could vary drastically in any particular week, month, or year. However, over time, with the right processes in place, we have found if properly priced, you will win on the majority of clients.

Team members. Same goes here. Team members are not all created equal. Some team members are new, some are old. Some team members comprehend things better than others. There are numerous differences in team members. So, it is really hard to determine what the capacity of each team member is going to be.

Your team has a limited amount of resources — time and technology. With time, you would hope that over time your team would get better and more efficient with each client. Why would this happen? We have found that the longer the team member knows the client, the more efficient the team member becomes. The team member develops processes to make their job more efficient. The better the processes, the more work the team member can perform without the help of others. In theory, the team member's capacity should increase in correlation with the aging relationship of the client and the team member.

That does not include adding junior team members and additional technology. If the team member can leverage additional team members along with additional technology, they should see a significant increase in their capacity potential.

Tasks. Unfortunately, the time it takes to perform tasks is also going to vary significantly from client to client. It is also going to vary from day to day. A bank reconciliation during the client's peak season is going to take longer to perform than a bank reconciliation that is performed during a non-peak season. You are never going to get it right 100% because there are just too many variables that have to be accounted for.

We have found that the gross profit for service-based businesses in growth mode runs consistently around 45 to 50%. Where a service based business that is experiencing flat growth with a lot of tenure in both their team members and clients is going to maintain roughly a 50 to 55% plus gross profit.

That being said, you should be able to accurately calculate the average bill rate for the clients and effective rate of the employee. Don't take them at face value until you have a couple of years to analyze trends. Assuming that you priced your product right, you should see an increase in both over time as the client relationship ages and the team member grows in experience.

It sounds simple, and it is. With value-based billing, you are going to win some and you are going to lose some. The better you can manage your clients, team members, and tasks, the more the scale will tip in your favor. But when you think about it, isn't that what you are supposed to be doing no matter how you bill?

Chapter 5: Predicting Profits – Profit Metrics #3

"When we sit down to look at these numbers together, it can totally change the way you run your business. We help you see things in a whole new light." - Jody Grunden

We have a saying in accounting: Profits are good. We like to see lots of our clients report lots of profits. So how profitable is your company? You probably think you know the answer to that, but don't be so sure.

Let's start with the basics. Just what is profitability? It's your bottom line. It's what's left after you add up all of your revenue and then subtract all of your expenses, including what you pay yourself. That's where a lot of companies miscalculate — they don't include the owner's salary in expenses, they think it's part of the profits. Wrong! You need to pay yourself, and you need to pay yourself well. If you aren't doing that, why are you taking all the risks that come with owning a company? Paying yourself should be a significant expense. Okay, end of lecture.

The bottom line on your bottom line is this: revenue minus expenses. So now you know. But that's just a number — it may be a big number, but it's a raw number, and that's not as important as a percentage. While many business owners know the dollar amount of their profits, not nearly enough know the percentage. And very few know where that number should be.

Take your bottom line net income amount and divide it by the top line gross revenue amount. That's your profitability percentage. What's your number? Is it 5%? That's not very good. 10%? That's better. But you should always strive toward 15-20% on a regular annual basis. Bear in mind your profitability will vary from month to month because your income and expenses will vary, but your annual number should be 15-20%. If it's more than that, congratulations. You're very profitable. If it's less than 10%, you're still in the black, which is much better than being in the red, but you have work to do.

Let's crunch the numbers. If your company has $2 million of annual revenue, you'd want $300,000 to $400,000 in profits. Again, that's after taking the owner's salary into account.

Speaking of your salary, what expense category are you in? Let me back up for a second, how do you break out your expenses? Do you break them out properly? Basically, with expenses, there are four big buckets: production expenses, administrative expenses, marketing expenses and facility expenses. The production bucket includes all the production employees — people that are actually working in the job, producing revenue. That's not just their salary, it also includes their health insurance,401(k) and other benefits, continuing education, technology, all costs directly related to that employee. Administrative expenses would also include employees, but they're the ones whose costs are coming out of your pocket, not being billed to clients. Marketing would include marketing and sales employees along with all other expenses in that area. Facility expenses are obvious — rent, utilities, etc. We've found, on average, 30 to 35% of a company's overall revenue goes toward administrative, marketing, and facility expenses. The rest goes through production. Whatever's left after that would be the profit, which is separate from the owner's salary. Back to that for a minute. Where would you classify your salary — Production? Administrative? Marketing? Split between two or three buckets? You should know that. And you should know what's in your expense buckets.

Here's another important question: Do you know who your most profitable clients are? When we ask our clients that question, right away they point to their biggest clients, the ones who pay them the most money. And guess what? That's often the wrong answer. It's easy to get confused on this. You look at the top line revenue and think that's the main driver of a company's success. In reality, it's not. The key driver is actually the gross profit, which is the revenue minus the direct expenses related to that client. It's easy to look at a client who's providing a lot of revenue and think that client is really helping you. And they may be temporarily helping your cash flow, but remember, expenses are going to hit in the same area. A high gross profit client is going to help your cash flow and your overall profitability. When you analyze your clients, you may be very surprised to learn which ones are your most profitable.

On the other hand, you certainly should know which clients are the biggest drain on your resources. You can physically see that because you're utilizing all your team on that project. That's generally a good indicator — how much time are you actually spending on a project? Is it to the extent that it actually takes a big bite out of the profits from that client, or even becomes a negative? If companies don't analyze their gross profit from clients on a regular basis, they can be in for an unpleasant surprise at the end of the year.

Of course, one of the best ways to be more profitable is to make sure you're charging the right prices. Not charging enough is one the biggest profit killers. Sometimes companies put out a low quote because they really want that client or need the business, but too many times companies put out a low quote because they just don't know what the right quote should be.

Determining what to charge a client can often be more difficult than getting the job done. It's something we deal with regularly with our clients. It's actually a fairly simple process, once they know what goes into it. You have to identify two key factors. One, how much are the producers costing you? That's all costs associated with those employees, as we explained earlier. Then you have to figure out what profit margin you need from that client in order to generate the cash flow your company needs. Bear in mind, you have other expenses in addition to that team, as we mentioned earlier — administrative costs, overhead, etc.

Once you know the profit margin you need, you can come up with your sales price. But, don't stop there. Too many businesses stop there. We are often terrible at estimating our time. Oftentimes business owners have write-downs as much as 25%, so let's plan for those write-downs. You need to do that a little bit for overages, but no less than 10%. That will determine the sales price that you absolutely have to have on each of your jobs, assuming, of course, that everybody is at full capacity for the year. That's the next thing you look at — what type of utilization you're actually getting from your team. Now you have to go back in and create an additional cushion from that. Remember when I said it's a simple process? It really isn't all that simple. You have to go step by step backward from the profit percentage you need, the cost of your employees, and the sales price derived from that cost in order to see that profit percentage, and then an additional reserve on top of that for overages. But the good news is, once you've done all that, you've come up with the right price. No more winging it.

Undercharging isn't the only big profit killer. Under-utilization is another biggie. This is why it's so important to track time and productivity. If you're under-utilizing a team on the production side or you've under-estimated a job and know they're doing a lot of extra work or re-working what they've already done, that's taking a big bite out of your profits. Remember, your goal is to have your average bill rate as close as possible to your standard bill rate. But when an employee's average billable hour is below what you quoted for that job, there go your profits. One of the reasons this is so critical is that often, when companies are looking to improve their bottom line, they look at cutting costs, usually in the administrative or marketing buckets. But in reality, improving the utilization on the production side will have a much bigger impact.

Let's go back to the big picture. You probably know your total profits for the last year. Maybe you even know your profit margin. But what about the monthly profits and the monthly margin? Do you know how it broke down last year on a month-by-month basis? Do you have a good sense of how it will break down during the next year? If you can't answer those questions, you're far from alone. Most companies don't know where they're at on a month-to-month basis or a year-to-date basis, or a 12-month basis. Those are all the different things that a company should be well aware of. That's because the past helps predict the future. The importance of these numbers is to help you look at trends, see why expenses are going up or down, and try to figure out if there's any way you can curb the expenses that are impacting your bottom line. On the production side, can you hit the revenue size that you need to hit? If you're doing a forecast, is it accurate or does it need to be adjusted? If you aren't doing a forecast, how do you get started and how do you do it accurately?

Bear in mind, while the past is static, the forecast is always dynamic. It's changing every single month. As you increase or decrease producers, your revenue each month would also increase. If you lose a client, then you may have to adjust your forecast to account for the lost revenue. Or there might be a month where you have fewer employee workdays available. Holidays, vacations, company retreats and so forth will all have an impact on your top-line revenue. Expenses, on the other hand, are fairly static, but there are months where that number is also going to go up or down. So, when you do the forecast, consider this: You may not be profitable every month, but that's okay as long as you're prepared for it and you're profitable enough in the other months to make up for it. If you're forecasting a month where you're $30,000 in the red, as long as you have enough cash on hand to cover your expenses, you'll be fine. The problem is when you're not prepared for that loss or you're forecasting $60,000 in profits and you end up with a $30,000 loss.

Billing — how you invoice your clients and how you pay your bills — can also seriously impact your profits and, ultimately, your cash flow. Let's start with your clients. When you put together the proposal, the terms of payment should be spelled out clearly. You may need to negotiate them to get what's best for you. Maybe the client prefers a 45-day term, but a 30-day term is best for you, so you might reduce the sales price a little to get what you want. Then, of course, it's really important that the client pay those invoices on time. Make sure everything is correct on your invoice because if there's a discrepancy to be resolved or it goes to the wrong department or wasn't signed properly by someone, those are all legitimate reasons for delayed payment. On the other hand, some clients just pay late. If you know this in advance, make sure that you build that into the customer price. It's really important to stay on top of your accounts receivable — don't let them get out of control. Maybe you should send out a reminder after the invoice is past due for five days. Maybe if it gets to 15 days and you've already made that gentle reminder, it's time to get someone personally involved. You certainly don't want it to reach 30 days or longer. You're doing the work for the client, you've paid the labor expense already, you really don't want to reach the point where you have to pull the trigger and halt the work. This is your cash flow we're talking about.

The same goes for paying your own bills. Should you be looking at a quarterly payment instead of monthly? Do annual payments make the most sense? This really comes back to your forecasting. Do you know what your bottom line is going to be and what your cash is going to be going forward? You can dictate whether you want to pay something early, like an annual payment. Insurance is an example of something where making a yearly payment can save you on your yearly costs. Some vendors will give you a discount for paying quarterly instead of monthly. Some of your expenses need to be paid monthly.

When we sit down to look at these numbers together, it can totally change the way you run your business. We help you see things in a whole new light. It can give you a much clearer picture of what you need to actually accomplish in order to achieve your end goals. When you know just what your profit margin is and you have an accurate forecast of what it will be in the months to come, and more important, you know that it's not where it should be, then it's time to start pulling those levers we mentioned in Chapter 4.

Let's say you pull the weekly Expectation lever. You increase your weekly expectation by just two hours. Let's say your company does $3.5 million in annual revenue, and your employees bill 30 hours a week. If you can increase that number by just two hours, to 32 hours, that's going to generate an additional $200,000 in profits. $200,000 for two hours. That's pretty good. And that's something we've helped many clients achieve. Or maybe you get your average bill rate closer to the standard bill rate. Once again, a little change can have a huge impact. Let's say that same company has a standard price of $150 per hour. But they usually only get $130 because of write-downs. What if they could increase it just $5 to $135 per hour. That's going to add another $95,000 in profits. As I said earlier, without a good handle on your profit and your profit margin, you could be way off on what you're charging.

The flip side is when you look at all of this, you might decide NOT to move forward on something because you learn just how much it will cost. Let's say a company with 15 full-time equivalent employees wants to reward them and give everyone an additional week of vacation. That would actually subtract $78,000 from their profits. Oops.

All this talk about profits always comes back to one thing. Forecasting. It helps you know what your goal is and what it should be. Where you'll be next month, three months from now, a year from now. Without knowing that, you're more or less wandering in the desert, making decisions without a clear idea of what kind of impact and long-term effect they'll have.

You want — and need — safety, security. You don't want surprises. Knowing your profit margin and knowing where it will be down the road gives you the information you need to make sure your company's future is what it should be.

Chapter 6: An Accurate Forecast

"By having a forecast, you can begin to set aside money earlier so that it's not such a shock to your cash flow. That's probably been the biggest impact of having a forecast." - Matt Westgate

How many times have you made or changed your outdoor plans because of the weather forecast on TV only to have that forecast be wrong? Your picnic ends up getting rained out or you spend a beautiful sunny day indoors. We complain all the time about inaccurate forecasts. "Those guys have millions of dollars in technology and they still can't tell me if it's going to rain or not." When a forecast is wrong, it impacts people.

So, let's talk about your forecast. The one for your company. Do you do one? How often do you check it? How often do you revise it? How accurate is it? That kind of forecast can have a much bigger impact than a rained-out cookout.

A lot of business owners don't do a forecast because they don't see the importance of it. That's because they don't understand just what forecasting actually means. A lot of people think forecasting is something you do in November or December. You set up the entire year and then compare what you do to what you thought you were going to do. Wrong!

In reality, that's just part of it. That's the initial stage, but there's much more to it.   A true forecast is dynamic, not static. A forecast is going to be looked at and revised every single month, often many times throughout the month based on what you know. A forecast should be a prediction, not a guess. So as soon as you have more information, more facts, you need to put that into the forecast so that it can generate a real-time outcome for you.

Why don't more people realize that it's that important? It starts with understanding how to put a forecast together. I often hear, "Well, our sales vary from month to month so there's no way I could actually put together something that would mean anything." That's completely false. As we've shown before with the KPIs, you can easily put together what you should expect your team to have based on what your team can produce. Then, look at what you have under contract and compare that with what is in your pipeline. This should give you a confidence in what your team may or may not perform over the next few months. Will you maintain, will you exceed, or will you fall short?

And your forecast prepares you for virtually every major decision you can make — expansions, acquisitions, buyouts, retirements. It's a tool to guide your future. I met with a client just the other day who said, "We are looking to buy out a competitor's business." Can this type of thing actually be accomplished? The deal could be perfect in every way as deals go; However, it might not be the right deal at the right time. We needed to look into whether or not they had their cash reserve built up. If so, then they may be able to take the risk. If not, then the risk may be too great and we would have to pass. The deal was the same in both scenarios, but it came down to whether they could absorb the risk based on how much cash that they had in reserve.

A good forecast should have the ability to be dynamic so you can input or integrate different scenarios. When would be the best time for a partner buyout or maybe the acquisition of a company? How would going from hourly billing to flat-fee billing impact the bottom line? All of these should be accomplished through proper forecasting. That's the real importance of forecasting. You can use it as a tool to guide your future.

Many of my clients ask me the difference between forecasting and budgeting. Budgeting is static. Budgeting is where you look and say, "Here's the amount of money I'm going to spend in this category and that category." And, that doesn't usually change, or, if it does, it doesn't change much. A forecast is constantly looking forward and making changes based on what happens. You need to consider things like how many new employees you need to have when we land a big project or how that will impact cash four months from now. A budget is simply a fixed number. How much are you going to spend for office supplies this year? It's important that your forecast has good budgeted numbers to work with, but if the numbers change, so does the forecast.

Todd Nienkerk:

> *Forecasting is probably the biggest single thing we've benefited from. That, and the ability to game plan. Working with our CFO and his team, we're able to set up long-term revenue goals to say, "Okay, between two and five million dollars of revenue annually." Any company is going to struggle because you've reached a*

stair step in the business where you have to increase administrative overhead, but you're not increasing productivity or production. You're just taking on more expenses in order to grow. It's such a cliché, but you have to spend money to make money. You have to hire administrative people in order to make more money in the future, to keep the ship running. Between two and five million, you're kind of stuck in that zone. We had been stuck in that zone for years, but we're finally crawling our way out of it. The fact that an expert can tell us, "Oh, these struggles that you're dealing with? This feeling of, why do we feel like we're on this treadmill? It's because of this. It's because you haven't broken through this barrier. You need to either be sub two million, or you have to be greater than five. But in between is hard." That kind of goal setting, and then being able to plan for that and create goals around growth to break past the walls, that's, I think, the second most important thing that accurate forecasting does for us.

What goes into a forecast and how far should you forecast? You should always look at least one year out. At my company, we actually look 10 years out, if not more. But that's just us. Most companies can get away with just looking at least one year ahead. And within the year, you're looking at revenue, production employees, what type of revenue they can drive, and what their expenses will be. All of that leads you to gross profit. Then you want to dive into all the different areas you can control like marketing expenses, administrative expenses, and facility expenses. Once we have identified what the expenses are and how much they will be, we look at the timing of those expenses. You may have certain expenses that are higher in certain months. Then we plot out exactly when we think things are going to occur. Are they going to occur monthly, every other month, or just annually?

Now let's back up and take a look at the revenue. We don't just take the yearly number and spread it out equally among 12 months. We take a look at utilization on a month-by-month basis and determine revenue based on those calculations. You may have months where you're heavy in vacations or your team will be at a conference or the month has a couple of holidays. You want to be sure you have a realistic number for the entire year, but also month by month.

How often should you be looking at your forecast? At least on a monthly basis. Once a month is the minimum frequency that you'd want to look at a forecast to get the most out of it. If you don't, you're going to run into issues where you'll end up saying, "If I had known this or that, I never would have made that decision." Or maybe you should have moved forward on something that you passed on and ended up missing out on a great opportunity. What the forecast really does is provide you the ramifications of everything and gives you the tool you need to make informed decisions. Looking at the forecast before every important decision is imperative.

Let's take another look. Let's say you go through this process and you determine you have forecasted an average bill rate of $150 next month based on your current team, but because of all the rework that your team has been doing, you know that you will end up with an average rate of $100, not $150. So you need to go back to the forecast and change the assumptions to see how they impact the financials. Now you're looking at a potential forecasted revenue shortfall, which you can live with if you're prepared for it. You know this because the following month is going to be strong based on what you know and what your forecast is telling you.

Your revenue is going to fluctuate, perhaps significantly. If you're a $3 million company, you aren't going to have a steady quarter of a million dollars coming in every month. At the same time, your expenses will fluctuate too. Some are fixed, like your rent or mortgage and your payroll, but you pay your taxes quarterly. And you might have a month with a conference that will cost you tens of thousands of dollars. The benefit to forecasting is knowing the highs and the lows and knowing that the highs are high enough so that when there is a low, you're going to be okay.

Lori Gold Patterson:

> *Here's how forecasting has helped us. We had a banner year this year. When we were only about three months into the engagement, we had already built our cash reserve back up. We were just having a banner, banner year. But in October, one of our largest clients suddenly had to put a complete stop on their spending. We had a week's notice. We also had about half of our utilization tied up in that project. All businesses that are in this industry have had that situation. Then you have to try to figure out, "Okay, how is that going to impact us? What's going to happen down the road? How quickly do we need to work? What type of work?*

How much time do we have? What do we have in the pipeline?" All of the questions that you start asking yourself create a very stressful situation when things like this happen. But this one wasn't stressful because we now had a dynamic forecast in place. We adjusted the entire forecast based on our new actuals. We were able to see the numbers and see the graphs, and see exactly how we were going to finish the year. We pulled in clients that we hadn't had capacity for before and did all the things we would normally have done, but without any of the stress. We had none of the stress that has always happened in the past. I didn't have to try to calm people down, tell them that it's okay, or make people nervous by saying that it wasn't okay. I wasn't having to drive any of that. I wasn't having to try to get everybody to understand the situation that we're in while I'm trying to figure the situation out myself. I didn't have to do any of that. All of that was just mapped out for us. Every week we adjusted it. We're in good shape, and none of us got any gray hair through that process.

With the pipeline, you're looking at contract to capacity, what your expected revenue is going to be, and what you have under contract. To get the percentage, simply divide contracted revenue by team capacity. We're looking at that on a regular basis. Once we've determined what our revenue is going to be — because it's different every single month based on company culture, holidays, etc. — it's important to know month by month what your expected revenue is going to be and then look at your pipeline to see if you can support that revenue. It's basically a formulated amount.

It is extremely important to be honest with yourself about the quality of your pipeline because your pipeline is simply a list of potential prospects. What dollar amount is associated with them? That's the key question. When I look at them, I take out the outliers, the ones that are way high or way low and are going to really distort things. Once you take out the outliers, you have a pretty good idea of the total potential revenue in the pipeline. Then you have to factor in how long it takes to close a deal that is in the pipeline. From start to finish, you want to see where that pipeline is from the day the lead became a qualified lead to the day you actually start working on it. That's an important number to help you determine how much money you need in your pipeline at all times.

For example, maybe you're expecting $300,000 in revenue. Maybe your pipeline needs to be $1 million to support the $300,000. If the pipeline is only half of that, you know there is a very good probability that you are not going to hit your expected revenue numbers. Unless something drops into your lap, your producers aren't going to be able to produce what you need. That's not good, but you can brace for it and make the necessary decisions. It could be a short-term decision, where jobs are falling off and you now have extra capacity. Or it could be happening this month, next month, every single month and now you have a long-term situation. That could mean you have to eliminate positions. Or maybe certain departments aren't pulling their weight and you need to reassign some people.

Whatever it is, you have to deal with it. Sometimes the forecast shows that you're not where you wanted to be, but you're still getting good results. You're still building cash, you're still meeting key numbers, and that's okay. But if it's not acceptable, that's when you have to make a tough decision. Maybe you need to let one of your producers go or maybe you need to hire another marketing person to help generate additional revenue.

As I said earlier, very few small business owners really do a forecast. When we do one with a client for the first time, often they'll look at it and wonder how we actually put it together. Keep in mind that a forecast helps us determine what cash is going to look like over the next month, so we break down the math behind it. "Here are your accounts receivable, 45-day terms are common for the marketing industry, but your clients are hitting 60 days, so here's what it looks like based on the 60-day spread. Here's what your cash is going to look like. Here's what your accounts receivable is going to look like." We start breaking down all the different factors and show them the net income we expect them to have month by month and what their cash balance should be during the same period.

Unfortunately, not everyone gets it the first time. Some people don't really get it until they've been through it three or four times — maybe five or six times for some people. And some people just never get it. That's where the person who oversees the financials is critical to the organization. They're looking at these numbers and breaking out the forecast on a regular basis so they can see where the cash is going to be. It really does all begin and end with cash.

We talked a lot about cash in Chapter 1. Remember, the need for cash on hand will vary from client to client. It's not a "one size fits all." It's a pretty clear formula. You always need at least a minimum of 10% of revenue. That's 10% of the last 12 months and that's assuming the business is flat or slightly growing. If the business is on a high growth rate, then you may need to increase the percentage to 15% to help manage growth.

Then you look at what else is going to happen going forward. Are you acquiring a building? You're going to need some cash for that. Maybe you build up to 12.5% or 15%. If you're getting to the point where a partner is going to be leaving in the next few years, let's start building cash for it now. Worried the economy is going to fall apart? Then maybe you need closer to 30%. As I mentioned earlier, I think anything over 30% is probably overkill. Having 10% to 30% of revenue in cash equates to approximately two to six months of expenses, which comes back to your forecast. What is your forecasted revenue and what are your forecasted expenses?

Matt Westgate:

> *Changing from budgeting to forecasting helped us with our yearly retreat. In previous years, we would just do it. We would do it and try to make sure that we had enough money so we could, or we would just dip into the line of credit. Now we can sit down and say "We're pretty much committed to doing a retreat every year.*

How much do they cost? When's the best time of the year to do them so that we're not disturbing our clients so much and so that our cash flow is good too?" Being able to look at the forecast and see what those expenses are going to be and then true them up every month against the forecast is really, really valuable. Part of it is just coming from a cash flow perspective. You can't save for something when you don't know how much it's going to cost. By having a forecast, you can begin to set aside money earlier so that it's not such a shock to your cash flow. That's probably been the biggest impact of having a forecast.

Don't forget to pay very close attention to the cash flow side. One of the benefits of forecasting is you have a clear picture of how your clients pay you. You might say, "Look at this, our biggest client always pays two weeks late." The forecasting gives you a clearer picture of how those extra two weeks impact cash.

If you're highly concentrated in any client, then it's important to have more money in the bank. By "highly concentrated," I mean 10% or more of your revenue comes from one client. This creates a risk that would warrant raising the cash reserve to 12 to 15%. The reason being, if you suddenly lose that client, you are going to have a lot of producers sitting on the bench not generating income. Also, when are those highly concentrated clients paying you? If your highly concentrated clients are also paying 60 days late or on 60-day terms versus 15-day terms, then I would adjust that cash reserve percentage even higher.

Of course, there's a benefit to knowing that in advance. It can change the way you pay your bills. Maybe you need to create new terms for your vendors. You don't have a lot of options. You can use your cash or you can use your line of credit or you can change how, and how often, you pay your bills.

Your biggest expense is probably your human capital — your staffing. It's critical to do proper forecasting because it puts you in a position of knowing that three months down the road you could be seriously short staffed. Or, three months down the road you could be in a position where you aren't going to be able to make payroll. Also, how you utilize your people is another big difference between forecasting and budgeting. Say your payroll is $40,000 a month. That's $480,000 you're going to spend over the course of a calendar year. But if your income is fluctuating and your work is fluctuating, your staffing may need to fluctuate as well.

There's so much that goes into forecasting and so many things that it impacts. The next time you complain because that the weatherman got it wrong and you got rained out, think about your own forecast. Do you have one? Is it accurate? What's your outlook?

Chapter 7: Pulling Levers 1 & 2

"One of the fun parts of my job is showing this to a new client and watching their eyes get bigger and bigger." - Jody Grunden

Recently, a friend of mine took a Caribbean cruise. For a week, he played the dollar slots in the ship's casino. At the end of the week, he was within a few dollars of being dead even, and he was happy. Sure, he would have liked to have won a few hundred dollars, but pulling those slot machine levers for a week kept him entertained and didn't cost him anything.

For you and your company, pulling levers can do a lot more than keep you entertained or earn you a few hundred bucks. It can impact your bottom line by hundreds of thousands of dollars. Back in Chapter 4, we outlined the four production levers you can pull. Now let's start pulling them!

In this chapter, we're going to look at Levers 1 and 2. Lever 1 is Utilization. It's your all-encompassing lever. Lever 2 is Weekly Expectation. That's going to help determine what your utilization rate ends up being. It's going to take things like your company culture into account and establish just what you expect out of your team each week.

One important point here. When we're talking about your team, we're talking about the production team only, not your marketing and sales team and not your administrative team.

For utilization and weekly expectation, we are only looking at people who are directly billable to a client.

Lori Gold Patterson:

> *Before I left, we had come out of an exceptionally busy time. There were some internal projects that count as our dream projects that we wanted to work on. We had the financial strength to do that, so we had turned our attention to those internal projects. That was going to go on for a short period of time, while we built up our pipeline. But I left, and they stayed doing those projects. We had a new business development person, and he was being told that everybody was too busy. They were busy, but they weren't busy on billables, so our utilization went down to about 15% — just terrible. When I came back and recognized it, we ramped up very, very quickly, and we got ourselves back to our normal operating utilization.*

So, what's your expectation? For instance, on a 40-hour work week, some people expect their team to bill 40 hours. But if they're billing 40 hours, that means they're working more than a 40-hour week, which indicates what type of culture that company is trying to build. It's a cash culture. Which is going to lead to turnover because people can't sustain that high of an expectation. On the other hand, some companies go the opposite direction. They say, "You know what? I want people to really enjoy life, and I want them to bill 28 hours a week out of a 40-hour work week." Employees might love that, but that's also not really sustainable on the business side because the revenue just isn't there.

There's really a fine line when it comes to company culture. Companies need to decide if they want to be that really cool "it's fun to work here" kind of company or if they want to be the "I have to bust my butt here" kind of company. There are different people and different companies that fit both models, so we can't say either one is right or wrong. It's just a matter of whether they can be sustained.

What we find is that most people are somewhere in the middle. They fall in the bucket of about 32 to 34 hours a week that they expect their people to work while they're actually billing clients. That's just billable hours and it's based on a normal week — no vacations, no holidays, no sick days, nothing outside the norm. Your weekly expectation is what you expect each person to bill to clients on an average week.

What does utilization take into account? It starts with the weekly expectation but then looks at things like vacation days, holidays, sick days, and days when people can't work because they're at a training session, a conference, or a company retreat. Here's what we call all that other stuff: the other stuff. Utilization takes into account anything and everything based upon the environment of the company, or the company culture.

Lori Gold Patterson:

> *Because we had been in such bad shape when I came back from being ill, everybody was working at top capacity. We'd put a lot of insistence on our billables. "How many hours have you billed this day, this week?"*

But with our company culture, when we're that heavy on our utilization, it feels yucky. It feels like we're not focused on the right thing, which is providing innovative approaches to our clients' problems. People were starting to get disgruntled, and justifiably because we had such a focus on billable hours. That was the only way we were going to make payroll because we had so little money when I first came back. We'd been operating for about three months at that top capacity, and we were pouring money into our reserves, and everything was going really well.

I knew we had to keep up that level of performance but somehow bring back our culture. So, I met with our CFO, and said, "I want you to change all our utilization numbers. I want to reduce them by four hours a week for everybody. Show me what our forecast looks like." He was able to adjust all of that and very quickly show me that yes, this was unusual, but if I wanted to bring our utilization down like that, we would still be performing just fine. With that information and that confidence, we then introduced something that we call Foundation Fridays.

From 1:00 to 5:00 every Friday, the entire company is working on passion projects, they're doing cross-discipline projects. People are doing presentations and learning together. I would not have had the confidence to do that, or been able to convince my executive team that we could do this if I didn't have the CFO to show me and everybody else that the numbers were actually going to hold up. In fact, what happened was our utilization went up because people's stress level came down. The excitement about Fridays, being able to have a release for their creative energy, got everyone rejuvenated, and our utilization actually then went up.

I probably could have done it without the CFO, but I would have done it with a lot of bumps and bruises. I would have had to go through a whole lot to convince myself and others, and then try to prove it. I don't know that we would have been able to so comfortably sustain it, because if anything else had affected our finances, for example losing this client, the client losing their budget, we probably would have torn out Foundation Friday right away, because we would have expected that financially, we needed to do that. Because this was based on factual financial reporting and forecasting, when that project left, for example, we didn't touch Foundation Friday. It's still completely in place.

Your company culture really is all-encompassing, and it impacts everything you do. Take vacations for example: Do you offer two weeks, three weeks, four weeks, or unlimited? Do you have employees who don't get any vacation time? How many holidays do you offer? Maybe you have a company retreat every year, or you frequently send employees for training. Those are huge for many companies. You might have two weeks a year where an entire team can't bill a single hour, separate from vacations and other time off. Research and Development are important to some companies, but a Research & Development project can't be billed to a client, and it might never even materialize into actual revenue.

When we look at these two levers, it comes down to simple math. For weekly expectation, you take the number of weekly billable hours and divide that by 40 working hours in a week — pretty simple math. The utilization, on the other hand, is the annual billable hours divided by the available billable hours. You might ask, how do we calculate available billable hours? Let's say you pay an employee for 40 hours a week, including holidays, vacation, and everything else. You have them for 52 weeks. So, the simple math is 40 hours multiplied by 52 days or 2,080 hours. You then subtract all of your culture hours. We define culture hours as the hours that you do not require your team to bill (vacations, holidays, sick days, conferences, etc.). We add all of those hours up and subtract them from the 2,080 hours we just calculated. This amount is your **available billable hours**. We are not done yet. We take your available billable hours and multiply that by your weekly expectation. This amount is your total billable hours. So, we take billable hours and divide by the available hours. This ends up being the Utilization percentage.

Utilization will vary from month to month and company to company based on the culture of the company.

Matt Westgate:

> We've been able to get smart on money. We've been able to work very closely with the CFO to fine-tune the reports to the way that we needed to see them. When we started working with the CFO, we didn't even know what a KPI was. We hadn't even heard of that acronym before. The key performance indicators are basically

the most critical numbers that we need to see on a weekly or monthly basis. We were able to fine tune those to not just sit back and have Jody give us the data but to own the data ourselves and to make sure that we understand where the numbers are coming from. Every week, our CFO gives us a cash flow report. Once a month we all get on the phone together in a video share. My leadership team and me, there are six of us, we all get together and go through the numbers. Everybody owns their different department, and make sure that we're up to speed. Then, once every quarter, we do a written report to the team. We call it the Weather Report, and the CFO generates a report customized to our team so that they can see our revenue, our profits, things like that so that everybody's on the same page.

In simple terms, utilization has variables and weekly expectation does not. Weekly expectation is simply this: during a regular 40-hour work week, no vacations or anything, what do we expect an employee to work? Maybe you expect that employee to bill clients 32 hours, and spend the other eight hours on things like emails, marketing, education, administration, and so on. Or maybe you expect certain employees to do nothing but billable work for clients all week, and that's their norm for the entire year.

I hope I haven't lost you because now we're getting to the important part. Do you know your weekly expectation? Do you know your utilization rate? When we sit down with owners of companies and ask them their utilization, nine times out of ten they give us their weekly expectation. So, most companies know that number, but very few know how it impacts their bottom line numbers. And even fewer know what their true utilization rate is.

If a company is flying blind, they'll never know what this is, and they can never make truly informed decisions. But once they really get into the weeds and figure out what everybody's utilization is and then benchmark that against each other, it's a real eye-opener.

You see two people who are doing a similar type of work, but one person is doing it a lot quicker. Why is that? Is the one just doing a great job or does the other need some additional training? Or is the slower one doing such high-quality work you can live with the inefficiency? You might discover that employee X is doing A, B, and C very well and very efficiently, while employee Y is doing D, E, and F just as well, but neither is particularly good or efficient at the others.

It could lead to providing more education for certain employees or reassigning duties. It could lead to staffing changes, maybe hiring different people or letting people go. Both weekly expectation and utilization help you know what you have and what you should have and make the necessary changes, but utilization is the one that really helps you gauge your team and their expectations.

We've found that utilization varies widely from company to company, but the average is somewhere between 60% and 65%. This is where your company culture comes in. Obviously, there's higher utilization if the company is tighter with its cash. For example, if they give two weeks' vacation versus three or four or they don't have company retreats or they send their team out for continued education, those types of things. On the other hand, companies that give more vacations and have retreats can still have a high utilization rate if they tweak their weekly expectation.

But it all comes down to knowing the numbers. Remember, these are numbers that impact your bottom line, so a small change can have a big impact. Here's an example. When we crunched these numbers with a client, we discovered that they expected their team to work 32 billable hours a week, butut they didn't have the work for that. They had enough for 28 hours. So, they had two choices: get more work or let someone go. No one wants to get rid of a good employee, but there are times you have no choice. You have to do what makes the most sense, not based on emotion, based on numbers. That is what we call an informed decision.

Todd Nienkerk:

> *There was a time in early 2015 when we lost a really big job. For the first time in our history, we had to lay a couple of people off. Our CFO was able to guide us through those staffing changes and identify who we should let go from a financial perspective, who we could stand to lose from the financial perspective, and then how many people we'd have to let go. We were able to make staffing decisions based on that. We're also able to make staffing decisions from the hiring standpoint much more intelligently.*

Working with our CFO and a group called Payscale, which is a benefits and payroll database, we've been able to identify what is an appropriate salary for various positions. We didn't have that data before. Every salary was negotiated on a case-by-case basis, which led to some serious outliers, meaning people that were either paid way too little or way too much for the role that they were in. We were able to see through these numbers that yes, this person is 50% more productive than anybody else, they bill 50% more time, but you're also paying them 50% more, so it's a wash. You may think that you're getting extra out of this person, but because you're paying them more, it's actually the same as just having two people. Would it be less risky to just have two people? I'd say that we didn't let anybody go for that reason, but we have certainly adjusted our new hiring strategy around that idea.

Matt Westgate:

Probably one of the hardest things is when we had to do layoffs. The thing about keeping an eye on the numbers is you can start to see when things are starting to happen. We had a window, a four-week window where we knew that if we didn't get some work that we'd be having to look at layoffs. It gave us more time to prepare. We had more time to have conversations and play out different scenarios and have plan A, plan B, and plan C. As each week went by and we saw what the cash was and what the sales were, we could adjust our plan as necessary. Layoffs are never fun. One person said to me once that the moment it gets fun to let somebody go is probably also the moment you should step down as the CEO of your company because that means that you've lost touch with the humanity side.

Let's say your utilization is 60%. When you look at your forecast, you might discover you can reach your goals and be as profitable as you desire with that number. Or you might discover that you need 65%. So, you have changes to make. If your weekly expectation is 30 hours, changing that to 32 can have a huge impact, depending, of course, on how many people you have. The more people, the bigger the impact.

One of the fun parts of my job is showing this to a new client and watching their eyes get bigger and bigger. Especially when we take the forecast out and show them in real life terms how just making a small change like that has such a huge impact on cash. Remember, building cash is our biggest goal. Cash gives security to the company and the team when we sit down with a company and they tell us they have $50,000 in the bank and we start tweaking their utilization. We change a couple days, we change some billable hours, we show them how they're underutilizing certain people, and then all of a sudden — boom! They're going to have $350,000 in the bank. They didn't get any more clients. They didn't decrease their costs. They didn't increase their prices. They just changed what they expect their team to work on a weekly basis or an annual basis.

It works the other way, too. We save companies from making a really bad decision. We have companies come in and say, "Hey, we have 32, and we're thinking about making it closer to 28 or 29. What do you think?" We do the numbers, and say "No, you really don't want to do that." It's a good thing they came to us first and did the calculation before making their decision because once you've made a decision like that, it's really tough on morale to go back.

Think about your company for a minute. How many employees do you have? How many hours do they bill each week? What's your average bill rate? What if each employee billed one more hour each week? What would that do to your bottom line? It's a nice number, isn't it? And that's just one hour a week.

Speaking of your average bill rate, how close is it to your standard bill rate? How do you get it closer? How do you bump up your effective rate? Get ready to pull those levers next.

Chapter 8: Pulling Levers 3 & 4

"We didn't know what our average rate was. We had no idea. We didn't even know how to calculate that." - Matt Westgate

Billing. We all do it. We don't enjoy doing it, but if we don't bill our clients, they don't pay us. Sometimes they don't pay us when we do bill them, but that's another story. For now, let's look at your Standard Bill Rate and your Average Bill Rate. Do you know what they are? If you're lucky, they're the same, or at least darn close. But chances are that they are not. Standard bill rate is your goal, Average bill rate is reality. This is one of the reasons they're such important levers to pull when it comes to improving your bottom line.

Bear with me for a quick refresher course. Standard bill rate is what you charge for service. If you charge a client $175 per hour for a service, that is the standard bill rate. If you bill flat fee or day rate you will need to back into your standard rate. Divide the total fee by the number of estimated hours working on the project. If your standard bill rate is $800 per day and you're only working eight hours, then your standard bill rate here is $100 per hour. It's always based on the amount of time that you are billing a client. The standard rate assumes you are not going to have any write-ups or write-downs on the project.

The average bill rate takes into consideration the write-ups and write-downs. The average bill rate is the total revenue you billed divided by the total number of hours you billed. If your standard bill rate is $800 and you planned on taking eight hours for the project, then you're billing $100 per hour. But if you actually work for 10 hours on that day, your average bill rate would be lower than the $100. It would simply be calculated by taking $800 divided by 10 or $80. Therefore, you have a $20 or 20% write-down.

Your goal is to get your average bill rate as close to your standard bill rate as possible. Actually, your goal is to be right on the nose, but that never happens in any kind of service-based business. There's going to be a small write-up or a small write-down. If it's 10% or less, that's usually manageable. If it gets higher than 10%, then you know you're missing something. Often, we see write-downs in excess of 20% — ouch!

Matt Westgate:

> *We didn't know what our average rate was. We had no idea. We didn't even know how to calculate that. We didn't know how to factor in efficiency. People weren't logging their time on projects, so it's not like we could go back and look to see what billability was or anything like that. We had some projects where we had hours, but anything else that we did, whether it was fixed bid or retainer basis, we weren't logging our time for that. We didn't have a strong insight into our efficiency. We didn't have strong visibility into what our capacity was, either, as an organization. It was a pretty big change to get smart on that information. But a lot of companies, if they don't have these things, they try to institute them, but they don't always understand the why. That*

can cause a real schism among leadership and the rest of the team, if they're just being asked to do more busy work without a strong reasoning behind it.

Bear in mind, sometimes you're off on certain projects but overall, you're pretty close. It could be that your quote is off, or your people can't service the client in the time expected. One project could turn out to be much more efficient than expected. Another could be a "loss leader" where you knew there was going to be a 30-40% write-down but you wanted that project for a number of reasons. But if you're not tracking your average bill rate regularly and seeing how it compares to your standard rate, it makes accurate forecasting impossible. We base all our forecasting on the average bill rate.

So how do you calculate your average bill rate — by the job, the month, the week? Try all of the above. The average bill rate for the year is one number. It can vary month to month, week to week, or job to job. And it has a huge impact on your profitability. Your margin is where it's at. When you're doing your forecast, you're not just basing it on a pie in the sky number. You're basing it on historical information. What was your average bill rate in the past year? How did it fluctuate? You never forecast based on your standard bill rate. If you do that, you're going to be way off. And, I mean way off. And if you don't have an accurate forecast, you could be in serious trouble.

Many business owners don't realize the significance of getting their average bill rate as close as possible to the standard. It's such a huge lever that people can pull, increasing their revenue without increasing their prices. That's the first thing accountants generally say, "Well, you need to increase your price." But in reality, it's better to say "Well, that might be true, but it might be truer that you just have to improve your efficiencies and solve the issue of why you aren't hitting your standard price."

I mentioned that your average bill rate can vary job to job. It can also fluctuate by department, by team, by pricing structure, even by employee. Take departments, for example. You might find that your design people are taking longer than normal all the time. If your standard rate is $200 but your average rate for your design team is $150, you have a huge write-down there. Maybe your development team is getting things done quicker than expected so you could have a write-up. It might lead you to some efficiency training for members of a certain department or you might need to change the way you quote.

While standard is your goal, and average is reality, the fact is, the reality will change. This also helps you with your forecasting. Let's say your average bill rate for the last three months had a 10% write-down company-wide. That helps you plan for the next three months. Or perhaps you see that a certain project is causing significant write-downs because it's taking more hours or you did something wrong and there's a lot of re-work, but that project ends in a month, which should bump your average rate back up.

Many clients ask me if it matters whether they charge an hourly rate or a flat fee when it comes to pulling these levers. The answer is "no." What really matters is that you know what you're actually getting. But here's something to think about. A flat fee leaves your clients a lot more secure than you because they've agreed to a price and if the job takes longer than planned, that falls on you. Whereas when you bill hourly, the risk is always on the client. But for this purpose, the calculation is exactly the same.

We talked about bumping up the average rate. But another benefit of tracking this could be a change in your standard bill rate. You might bump it up to get more revenue or bump it down to get more clients. You can increase your standard rate or decrease it based on your average bill rate. Keep in mind, your average bill rate is tied to your forecast. If you keep it to the forecast, you can play with that standard rate all you want. It might be a different standard rate for each department. For example, design might be $250, development might be $200, and every other department might be a different rate.

How often should you track your average rate? I mentioned that it can fluctuate week to week. But don't bother tracking it that frequently because it can be distorted, depending on when clients are billed and things are earned. I recommend doing it on a monthly basis to give you an idea and then track it throughout the year. That's because it shouldn't fluctuate widely from one month to the next unless there are extenuating circumstances. It should be well within the range. If it falls off the tracks somewhere, that's where you go, dig in, and find out why it's off the tracks and whether you can fix it. Or is it going to be that way for a period of time? Now take a look at your forecast. If it's based on a higher number, you may need to make adjustments, at least on a monthly basis.

Your average rate and your standard rate are both important, obviously, but the key number is your effective rate. Here's your formula for that. Utilization percentage times the average bill rate. Or you take the revenue and divide that by the number of hours worked. Both formulas get you the exact same number, just different ways of getting there.

The effective rate is the all-in rate. It's the single most important number you have. You don't have to look at time, productivity, who's doing what, when, and for how long if your effective rate is in line with your forecast.

Remember, the bottom line from all these levers is the impact on your overall effective rate. Everything stems from that — your staffing levels, your capital purchases, how much the owner is paying themselves, all of that. This is why that rate is so important to understand — not only what it is, but what it should be, what the market is bearing, and more importantly how it compares to your forecast. You could be leaving a lot of money on the table. But you need to know just how your team is performing and how they should be performing.

This brings us back to your standard bill rate. What are you doing compared to your competition? While you have to look at yourself, you also have to look at the competition and the market. Some companies charge $125 an hour with a really small margin, barely getting by when they should be charging $175 an hour. Maybe Company XYZ gets double what you get.

If so, why is that? Is it because they have the reputation and you don't? Is it something you can get to? Knowing all the different factors helps you identify which levers to pull. Do you raise your standard rate? Do you work on your effective rate? Are you giving your employees too much time off or not enough? Do you add people or subtract?

Something else to think about: you might find that your average rate is right up there with your standard rate, but you're still leaving money on the table. If you're charging $125 and the average bill rate is $125 an hour, that's great. But what if you could be charging $200 an hour. You're leaving $75 an hour on the table. If you extrapolate that over what your team would bill for the year, that ends up being a pretty huge number.

Back to the question I asked at the beginning of this chapter: Do you know your standard bill rate and your average bill rate? Obviously, you know your standard rate. But when I meet with company owners and ask them their average bill rate, 100% of them will give me their standard rate. Then when we start looking at their average rate and see where it's off from the standard and by how much, they start seeing all those dollar signs floating away.

If you bumped your average bill rate up by $10 an hour, depending on the size of your company, it could mean an additional $200,000 to $300,000. We've seen significant swings with our clients by just making a small change. The biggest one was a company that was $300,000 into their line of credit. Once they began tracking all these numbers and pulling these levers, within two years they had a million dollars' cash in the bank. Cha-ching!

Once you have the roadmap, once you know where you're going, you basically have new goals that are easily attainable. It's a lot easier when you know how to do it. We see company owners who gain the confidence that was missing earlier. It's a game changer for them. Look, you know what you're doing when it comes to the creative side of things, but you're not a numbers person. Once you have the formula, you can make informed decisions, you have something to shoot for and you can attain it.

Chapter 9: Is your Pipeline Big Enough? – Pipeline Metrics

"If you forget about this metric, it can result a great situation turning into a bad situation — fast." - Jody Grunden

Once we have established how much cash we need in the bank, have put together a game plan to get there based on the Production Metrics and have determined that our profits are reasonable, then we turn to our pipeline. If you forget about this metric, it can result in a great situation turning into a bad situation — fast.

Our Pipeline is broken into two main parts. The first part is what you currently have under contract. The second part is what you have "in the works." Let's start with what you currently have under contract and compare that to what we have determined earlier was your capacity. We call this metric "Contract to Capacity."

Calculating this metric is relatively easy. We've already covered capacity, so now let's talk about how to determine what your team's capacity is month over month. Keeping in mind that each month's capacity is different based on company culture, the timing of new hires, and number of days in the month. Let's jump into how to determine what is under contract for each month. First, we will want to identify which accounts are recurring revenue. What I mean by this is we are going to get the same amount of money month over month on a perpetual basis. Once we have identified the accounts and the amounts, we will want to break them out month by month for the next six to twelve months. I recommend looking at this report for the next twelve months. However, keep in mind the only months that are crucial in this calculation are the next three months.

Once you have broken out the recurring revenue by month, then you are going to want to break up your contracted work by month. What do I mean by this? You will want to list all of your contracts in total and then try to determine in which months the work will be done. Did you read that correctly? I said you want to break down the contracts by when you believe the work will be done. This is not when you will invoice the work or collect the money.

So, let's say that Summit CPA Group just hired you to perform a job totaling $300K that will take three months to complete with 150 hours. When you look at the job, most of your time will be front-loaded in the first month. Let's say 100 hours. The remaining 50 hours will be spread evenly over the remaining two months. How would you recognize this revenue?

Open Jobs	Sep	Oct	Nov	Total
Walmart	0	0	0	0
Samsung	7,143	0	0	7,143
ExxonMobil	0	0	0	0
Apple	100,000	100,000	100,000	300,000
Toyota	15,000	0	0	15,000
BP	80,000	60,000	0	140,000
General Motors	0	0	0	0
Allianz	0	0	0	0
Summit CPA Group	50,000	0	0	50,000
Ford Motor Company	0	0	0	0
General Electric	0	0	0	0
Contracted Revenue	252,143	160,000	100,000	512,143
Contracted Revenue	**252,143**	**160,000**	**100,000**	**512,143**
Revenue Capacity	**276,096**	**317,929**	**184,064**	**778,089**
Contract to Capacity	**91%**	**50%**	**54%**	**66%**

It is pretty simple. From the facts above, we know that we are getting $200 per hour on this job ($300K divided by 150 hours). Since we are predicting 100 hours in month one, that translates to $200K in month one. The remaining 50 hours, or $100, is split evenly over the next two months. You would replicate this exercise for each job that you have under contract. When you are done you should have all of the work that you have under contract broken out by month over the next twelve months.

Now you have calculated what you have under contract for the next three months. Take that amount and divide it into what your total capacity is for that three months. This percentage that you calculate is going to be different from company to company.

Contracted Revenue	512,143
Revenue Capacity	/ 778,089
Contract to Capacity	**66%**

But, for all companies, the higher the percentage, the better. This quick calculation should give you a pretty good feeling of how accurate your revenue forecast is for the next three months.

Now let's take it one step further. How much do you have "in the works?" This part of the pipeline calculation can be broken down into multiple stages depending on how far you are in the courting relationship with new clients. For us, the courting relationship can last from one week to one year. Whoa — that is a long time! Well, not really. If you break the relationship down in segments it starts to make sense.

For this exercise, let's break down the pipeline in four segments. Segment one is prospect showed initial interest. Segment two can be when we gave the prospect the "why us" presentation. Segment three can be when we have given the prospect a basic quote. Segment four can be when we have given the prospect a formal quote. These are just examples of different segments. You can have more or fewer segments depending on whatever you typically find occurs during your sales approach. All of these segments need to be measurable.

Measurable for what? Each segment needs to be measurable in terms of the time the prospect takes to move from one segment to the next and eventually when the prospect is determined a client or a lost opportunity. Two metrics are determined here. One is your closing percentage. Simply put, the number of opportunities that enter your sales pipe that are converted into clients (Clients/Opportunities). The second is the days that it takes to convert a lead to a customer. The official term for this is the Average Sales Cycle.

Now the only other thing that you have to determine is what your average contract length is. This is the number of days that a typical contract lasts. You can look at historical numbers to determine that. Do the majority of your contracts last 30 days, 60 days, 90 days, 6 months or a year? This is a crucial number in determining if you have the right size pipeline.

Now that we have all of the elements of the formula, here it is:

PIPELINE NEEDED	
Revenue Capacity	778,089
Less Contracted Revenue	(512,143)
Revenue Needed	**265,946**
x Average Sales Cycle / Days Remaining in Period	60 / 90
x Average Contract Length / Days in Period	90 / 90
Close Percentage	/ 50%
Pipeline Needed	**354,595**

There were a couple of metrics we did not mention: Days Remaining in the Period and Days in the Period. Days in the Period are generally going to be 90 days because as I had mentioned earlier, you really only want to look 3 months or 90 days out at any time. And, depending on when you are looking at the pipeline, you may be at the beginning of the period, 30 days into the period, or maybe in the last 30 days of the period. The answer would be different in all three scenarios.

Now that you have determined the pipeline that you will need to meet your revenue goals, you should go back to your "dynamic forecast" and increase or decrease the months affected. If your pipeline adequately supports the forecast, then no adjustment is necessary. If it does not, adjust the revenue to better reflect your pipeline.

Chapter 10: Avoiding an Emergency Exit

"It'd be nice to take a few years off and then figure out something else to do. That's kind of the ultimate goal." - Todd Nienkerk

As we approach the end of the book, let's talk about your end game. What's your strategy? Do you have one? If not, you need one now.

In fact, the end game is something every business owner should think about from the very beginning. Why should you have one? Because you don't want to leave your company at any point unexpectedly in disarray. Think of it as your "hit by a bus" plan. You want to have a plan put together for the sake of your business and your family — especially your family. You don't want to leave them having to sort through everything if you were to pass away or have something drastic happen to you. You don't want to put that burden back on your family. This happens to companies all too often. An unexpected situation like disability or death of the owner is often the death knell for the company due to lack of planning. You want to protect yourself from retirement, death, and disability.

Okay, now that I've totally depressed you (and have you worried about crossing the street) let's look at this from a different perspective. You've built a good business, and it's going to keep growing. Someday, and you're going to decide when that is, you're going to want to sail off into the sunset with a big bundle of cash. That's a great end game. So how do you make it happen?

Todd Nienkerk:

> When we first started, we didn't have an exit strategy. Now, I think we have a couple. What I would like to see is to have Four Kitchens exist in the far future without me around. That would be the ideal outcome. That could be achieved by merging with another organization and leaving, or having it be acquired as a smaller shop, or the thing that I'm really interested in looking into this year is an employee-owned structure. Like an ESOP. How could we transfer ownership over to everybody else in the organization in a way that is sustainable for everybody, that provides my business partner Aaron and me with a longer-term retirement plan style buy-out over 10 to 20 years rather than three years? I'd say that my gut's telling me I've maybe got another five years left in me before I just totally burn out. By then, I'd like to be on my way to merging it with somebody else or finding an ESOP strategy or profit-sharing thing or something where I could just kind of take a few years off. It's not going to last me all the way. But it'd be nice to take a few years off and then figure out something else to do. That's kind of the ultimate goal.

Retirement, whether at 65 or 35 or somewhere in between, is the most common end game for business owners. Some sell to their partner or partners. Some sell to a bigger company or a competitor. Some sell to their employees. Some give the company to their employees. Some take a lump sum. Some take a 5 or 10 or 20-year payment plan. Some want their company to continue without them, some want it to be swallowed up.

But retirement isn't the only reason for a buyout. That in itself can be a pretty profitable end game strategy, whether you want to take the money and start a new company, go to work for someone else, or maybe cut back on work and kick back a little.

Whatever your end game might be, it's important to have a vision for it from the beginning. That doesn't mean it won't change. Just like any long-range plan, it's a living, breathing thing. You don't just write it up, throw it in a file drawer and forget about it for 30 years. As your business evolves, so should your end game strategy. Any change to your business plan will affect your exit plan. The top three drivers in valuing a business are financial performance, growth potential, and recurring revenue. How can you implement all three drivers into your current business model? Planning now is extremely important.

Matt Westgate:

> *I'm a big believer in giving everyone a stake in the outcome. When you're open and transparent, you're creating an ownership mentality in your company. People are smart. They don't want to show up to work just to do the work. They want to be a part of a community. The place that you work is a community,*

and if you like the people you're working with, then you want to keep it a place that's fun to work at and you want to grow it.

One of the things I would like to do is to take this whole ownership mentality to the next level. If I can, I like to teach, help people learn what the business is, how it works, the importance of taking an idea and having cash and customers behind the idea and proving that out, how critical that is. What I can do is when business opportunities arise, when adjacent business opportunities arise within our organization, I can say, "You. You are passionate about," whatever, conversational interfaces or robots to the moon or whatever it is. "You now have enough information to know what this thing needs to be to go be the next thing. Go start that business and we'll back you. You have the financial literacy. You have the business literacy," and I give people an ultimate promotion, a career trajectory that doesn't exist at most places where you reach the senior title and that's it. I don't want that at my company. I want to think that anybody can go be an owner, start a new business with the proper training and fundamentals. That's a big part of the ownership mentality for me.

In a way, it comes back to forecasting. But instead of looking ahead up to a year, you're looking ahead many years down the road. Often, it comes down to cash. Thinking about the company's needs after you're no longer there might lead you to build up your cash reserves as you lead up to that time. Maybe your cash reserve shouldn't be 10% any more. Maybe it should be 20% so there's less of a burden on the company in those first months after your departure.

How long have you had your company? How long do you think you'll have it? That answer is part of your exit strategy, if you don't already have one. Think back to the day you started your company. Chances are, the last thing on your mind was how you were planning to leave your company. But it really should have been. When we take on a new client and we ask them about their exit strategy, they usually respond by saying, "Shouldn't we be thinking about how we keep the company going?" But really the two go hand in hand.

So, you begin the strategy the day you open your company and then mold it as your company grows. Maybe you start off thinking, "This is only going to be me," so your exit strategy is a good life insurance policy to cover your wife and kids. But as your company grows and matures, you might start thinking about a partner. Do you bring on someone the same age as you? That may not be the best idea because you'll both be retiring at the same time. What about 10 years younger than you? That's a good idea. There's your succession plan. And if you keep growing, maybe bringing on a third partner 10 years younger than her. You're staggering retirement and setting the stage for buyouts. Or as your company gets bigger and bigger, maybe you start getting courted by other companies. Now your endgame is changing again. Having an end game plan is important. Changing it as your business changes is just as important.

It's also important to implement your strategy at the right time. If you wait too long, you're going to limit your opportunities. Let's say your goal isn't a lump sum buyout, but instead you want to have income from your company for five or ten years or whatever the buyout period is. If you don't start early, there's no way the company is going to be able to build to the level needed to pay you off. And consider this: If your exit strategy is to sell to a third party and you wait till you're about to retire, you're going to get the lowest dollar amount you can possibly get for your company because now you've given the buyers leverage. Know what your plan is, how to tackle that plan, and give yourself plenty of time to do it. That clock is ticking. Instead of a biological clock, think of it as a buyout clock.

Now that you're planning an exit strategy, here comes another biggie. What's your company worth? Chances are, it's less than you think. The fact is, most business owners overvalue what they think their company is worth. It's understandable, we have all this blood, sweat and tears built into our company, so we have an inflated view of its worth. But what is it actually worth to someone who might buy it? It's important to get a valuation done by a third party every so often. We actually have one prepared for our company every month because we can do it internally, just to see the ups and downs of it.

If you're looking to sell and you're banking on a $3 million sale, the last thing you want is to have your best offer come in at $1 million. You need to know the true value of your company, and the only way to do that is to use an independent third party. There are a lot of factors to look at. They have to look at much more than your P & L statements. What about risk? How will the company survive if you walk away? If it's without a hiccup, your company is worth a lot more than if you're a key pillar. What's your client base? If you have a lot of revenue but much of it is reliant on two or three huge clients instead of 10 or 20 midsized, your company is going to be worth a lot less because if one of those big clients leaves, where does that leave the new owner?

What kind of processes do you have in place? Do you have something of value that other companies don't have? That adds to your value. On the other hand, did you get seed money when you first started? That's going to lower your value.

What's your company culture? That's often driven by the owner of the company. Is it one that makes sense for you because it's the type of company you want to run even if it means lower profits? If a potential buyer believes in a totally different culture, either they're going to pass on buying your company, or they're going to lower their offer. Or they might going to blow things up when they take over, which would not be good for your company or your employees.

What type of company do you have? Is it distributed or is it brick-and-mortar? If you're distributed, are you trying to sell to a brick-and-mortar company that has no idea how to be distributed? There are many things to think about in order to make that sale work effectively.

Remember the levers we listed earlier in the book? Pulling them effectively does more than help your company be more profitable while you're running it. It helps you get more when you sell your company. If your average bill rate is close to your standard rate and your employees are productive and you're a $3 million company with 30 equal clients and your forecasts are solid and you're paying yourself a good salary, then you're putting yourself in a much better position to sell your company and get the price you want, if that becomes your goal.

Everything we've discussed so far is for a company with sole ownership, so, what about companies with multiple partners? For one thing, having multiple partners was part of the end game in the first place. Becoming an equity partner is an exit strategy. Now you have a tangible asset you can sell when you're ready to retire. But let's not go overboard. Some people come in thinking, "I want to be an equity partner because I'm going to make a lot more money each year," and they drain the company's cash every year. Guess what? Now the end game isn't going to be there when you want it. That shouldn't be the idea. The idea should be, "I want to be an equity partner so when it comes to the end, I have a retirement."

The end game is important to all the different partners, but it's really important going in to have the right motivation in becoming an equity partner. A lot of digital companies want to give a lot of their company to everybody else because they think everybody wants to be an equity partner. Well, they don't. Not everybody has the same dreams and goals that entrepreneurs have.   Sometimes that idea terrifies them. Don't be disillusioned by thinking everybody wants to be you because they don't.   Some people just want to be an employee, a team member. It's important to know your team, especially for the end game, because if you give away pieces of your company as you go and then find out people really don't want that, you've created a mess for yourself at the end.

If there are partners, that changes the whole dynamic of the exit strategy.   Obviously, there's the opportunity for the strategy of selling out to a partner.   A good buy-sell agreement is important to have any time you're bringing on a partner, whether it's a 50-50 split or you have a bunch of 2% or 5% partners. One of the reasons it's so important is that a business partnership is like a marriage. It can end in divorce. And divorces can be ugly.

So, as you've been reading this chapter, have you thought about what exit strategy makes sense for you? Selling to a partner?   Selling to a bigger company?   Selling to your employees?   Giving the company to your employees? Remember, your end game could change several times before you get to the finish line. What makes sense when you're 40 might look foolish at 50. What's fiscally sound for a $3 million company could be suicidal for a $10 million company.

What do you want to get out of it? Do you want an income stream or do you want a lump sum?   It all goes back to forecasting. Can you afford the lump sum? What's that lump sum going to be? How's it calculated? The bigger you get, the bigger that lump sum is going to be, so how much money do you have to actually have all the time? Those are the things you have to decide.   You also have to decide what's best for you, the owner, and what's best for the company. If what's best for you isn't best for the company, you may still make that choice. If you're a sole owner, it's your decision and it's your right to choose the option you want.

We have an exit strategy. And yes, I had one from day one. We modify it all the time. We look at it every couple of years and we make adjustments to it. We can think something is the dead-on way to do it and two years later it's not even remotely close to the right idea. It's like a living document — we go back and make adjustments, some of which are huge. If there's an agreement in place, it's binding, so if the circumstances and the strategy change, the agreement has to reflect that. We're going to continue to revisit it every couple of years and make changes as necessary.   Our goals have changed as our company has changed.

Let me tell you something we're doing, and why we're doing it. We used to keep a 10% cash reserve. Now we're going to build to 15% because we're thinking about bringing on some small equity partners, only a 1 or 2% percent stake. What if we make a mistake? What if things don't work out with one of them? We want to have the availability to buy that person out because we certainly don't want to keep someone on for five years if they aren't working out, so we need the option of a cash buyout that won't hurt the company. That may sound cold, but no one is perfect and we want to protect ourselves.

Back to the "hit by a bus" thing for a minute. I shudder when I think about all the business owners who can't answer the question of what would happen to their business if something happened to them. In my case, that's something I've planned for from day one. That's always been the goal, to develop a company where I could walk away tomorrow. The company is much bigger than just me. Everything I've done is with the idea that we develop it so I can be replaced. I try to hire team members that can replace me. If I'm good at something like servicing clients, then I try to get people that are better than me at servicing those clients. From day one, I've tried to build a team that I can walk away with, and so far, it's been really successful.

My partner is a great person who can succeed me. Maybe we bring on other partners who could potentially succeed him. We're always looking to pull us out of the equation, because if we can do that, then we know we've got a pretty solid company or solid processes in place. That's been the motivation. I didn't want to be the person working a gazillion hours in an accounting firm and having everybody rely on me all the way to the time I retire. There are certainly plenty of accounting firms like that. There are plenty of other businesses like that. It's just not for me.

Let me tell you about a client. The business had two partners. At one point, they were in trouble. They were deep into a line of credit. But we worked with them, and they recovered. Boy, did they. The business grew, and they both became replaceable. Now one of them is buying the other out. When the one being bought out told me about it, I congratulated him. He said "What do you mean, congratulations? I'm getting bought out." I said, "Yes, you built something out of thin air that's got value. How many people can do that?" He said "Wow. That makes sense." Now, he's getting a nice payout over time, a payout because of work he'd done. That's the beauty of it.

I think a lot of companies we work with start out where the owner is the producer. They don't want to be, but that's what they do best. But then the entrepreneur-type personality they've always had finally comes out, and they're able to work *on* the business instead of *inside* the business. Eventually they should be able to walk away and remove themselves from the picture because they have full control over it.

It can happen for you. And if you plan for it, it should happen. There's no reason why it won't, unless you're your own worst enemy, and then you can't get past that. It happens a lot, where business owners just don't believe they can get past it, and because they don't believe it, they don't do it. Have an exit strategy. Believe in it. Plan for it. And guess what? It will happen the way you plan.

Lori Gold Patterson:

> *I believe that when the CEO commands so much of the knowledge, the power, the control, your company is at best just sitting there at the edge of the cliff. One of the greatest things that has come from engaging our CFO and his team is that my whole executive team is as knowledgeable now. They have the same transparency. They can see, they can ask questions, they can help*

make the decisions. That empowers all of us. That strengthens our company so much that it's enabling me to go work on our company in many different ways instead of ensuring the financial.

Death and Disability should be taken into account at the formation of the business when putting together the buy/sell agreement. I am sure you have heard that during the course of your career you are way more likely to be disabled than to die. So, make sure that you address both. If you have not addressed both yet, it's not too late. Contact a business attorney and get a buy/sell agreement properly taken care of right away. The buy/sell agreement should address not only how the company will pay the partner, but also over what period of time.

How do you pay the partner? Ideally, your company was able to build enough cash reserve to pay the outgoing partner. If you do not have enough cash in the bank, then insurance can be the next best thing.

How can insurance help? For life insurance, there are generally two ways. One, the company can buy the insurance policy. Upon death, the company would receive the insurance proceeds and then buy out the deceased partner. Or two, both partners could buy policies on each other. Upon death, the insurance proceeds would then be used to buy out the other partner. Both have their pros and cons. You will want to rely on your accountant and insurance agent to determine the appropriate type of policy for your company.

How much insurance is enough? The correct amount is going to depend on how much your company is worth for life insurance and how much you are earning for disability insurance. How could you possibly know that? Disability is fairly straight forward – how much you are making. Life insurance is a little trickier.

The easiest way is to find out how much your company is worth is to get a valuation performed on your business. A valuation will give you an estimate of what an unrelated third party would purchase your company for. Once this amount is determined, you will have a good idea of how much insurance you are going to need now. What are you going to need in five years, ten years, and beyond? A periodic valuation would be a strong recommendation. It is going to be important that you constantly review your insurance needs so if the time comes your company will have enough money to pay the former partner's estate in the case of death, or the partner in case of disability. Whatever you decide, make sure your attorney includes the appropriate language in the buy/sell agreement to cover both scenarios.

So far, this chapter has been pretty self-centered. We have been talking a lot about how to deal with our departing from the company. We have not mentioned once what happens to your team. And, if you are anything like me, your team is your second family. So, I am going to devote the remainder of this chapter to that topic.

Often when looking for a way to reward your team outside of compensation, we often look at stock or stock options. I want to talk about both. I also want to throw out a couple of other options with phantom stock and phantom stock options. I am not going to go into great detail about any one of them, but I want to give you enough information to spark your interest. Let's talk first about stock.

Stock

Giving stock to key employees can be just what it takes to lock them in without adding compensation. Often key employees take pride in ownership, but with ownership, there comes a real cost. What do I mean by real cost? Money.

When giving stock to an employee, the employee has to either pay cash for the stock or recognize the value given in their compensation. Be very careful. Seek the advice of a CPA. Gifting stock to an employee could cause a very unexpected tax burden to the employee. And, depending on how much you were intending to give, the tax burden could be unaffordable for them. For instance, if your company was valued at $1 million and you decided to be generous and give your key employee 50% of the company in the form of stock, your employee would have to report on her taxes an additional revenue stream of $500K. Using a 40% tax rate, your employee would be the unexpected winner of approximately $200K in additional taxes – what!? Yep, you read it correctly – $200K in taxes. Your generous decision caused an unexpected tax burden of $200K. Not a good start for a new owner.

Stock Options

Stock options could be a more solid alternative than simply giving stock. When giving stock options, the employer is giving the employee the right to buy company stock at a specified price during a specified period. Assuming the value of the stock goes up, the employee can then exercise the stock option. The employee would buy the stock at the exercise price and sell the stock at the higher market value and then pocket the difference. This, of course, works only if the stock goes up. If the stock goes down, then the stock option is worthless.

Phantom Stock

Phantom stock and phantom stock options are very similar to stock and stock options with one very big difference — they are not true equity. Hmmm. Instead of equity, phantom stock is considered a form of compensation or cash bonus. Phantom stock gives the recipient the right to receive cash or real stock at a future point in time. That time is referred to as a triggering event. Generally, for most phantom stock plans, the triggering event is the sale of the company. Similar to stock, the value of the phantom stock is determined at the date the stock is given.

Phantom stock options are also a form of compensation. Similar to stock options, phantom stock options are a form of compensation or cash bonus given for the appreciation of the stock. Phantom stock and phantom stock options are ways to give a piece of the business to the employee without having the employee invest cash in the business or pay any unexpected taxes.

I am bringing all of these options to your attention for one purpose – to offer an opportunity for your employees to share in your exit strategy if you so choose.

Closing Thoughts

Okay, you made it through to the end. And your head didn't explode. Good for you. I know, there was a ton of information to absorb. So, what are you going to do with all that information?

I wrote this book so you can use it as a reference tool to go back to on a constant basis. Read it, re-read it, make sure you understand it and ask questions if you don't. It should give you all the tools you need to successfully manage the financial aspects of your business.

But tools only work if you use them. The levers we talked about only work if you pull them. Forecasting only works if you know how to do it right and know you have the right numbers to do it. It's up to you to put these tools in place, whether you feel you're the person to do it or if you have to hire someone to do it. That's a tough decision because it's a person that doesn't make you any money. The dreaded CFO.

But whether that person is internal or external, at some point you'll need to make that jump. Until you do, you'll never be the person who can walk away from your business. You trust yourself, as CEO, to run the company. You have to trust the COO to run the operations and the CFO to run the finances. Once you have everyone in place and you've gone through the process, and you know you can walk away, you've actually accomplished something greater than yourself.

That's really what I hope you get out of this book. "Hey, let's create a business bigger than us. Bigger than the names on the letterhead." I've outlined how to do it, through the forecasting, through the KPIs, through managing everything, through the planning, all that.

I keep coming back to forecasting. If there's one thing above all I hope you got out of this book, it's the importance of forecasting — how to create it, how to manage it, how to monitor it, and then why it's important to revisit it. You should revisit it every single week, every single month. You should do it regularly and rely on it. Every single decision you make should be based on the future.

Make sure you have enough cash in the bank. Make sure you have a pipeline that's strong. Make sure your people are working the way they should be working. Numbers don't lie. They take the emotion out of everything. If you're constantly looking over these things and monitoring them and making sure they're where they should be, you won't get hit with a big surprise. You'll be able to plan better. Planning should be the norm. Shift from reactive to pro-active.

It's been so rewarding for me to see this work for so many of our clients. To see them turn around and have the type of company they always wanted. Let me just give you an example. A new client came to us. They had no cash in the bank, they had major tax bills they weren't even aware they had to pay, and they had no money to pay them. They followed the steps in this book and we helped them turn it around. Now they have a very successful company and they have millions of dollars in the bank.

We also worked with a company that had a partner buyout. This one was a nasty business divorce. They brought us in as a temporary solution. Not only did they have no money in the bank, but they were completely tapped out on their line of credit to the tune of a million dollars. But the foundation was strong and once they started pulling levers, making changes and forecasting properly, we helped them completely turn things around. They now have well over a million dollars in the bank. The owner was able to start taking a salary of $200,000 a year. Now he's taking a salary of $600,000. And, on top of his salary, they're making about a million dollars a year in profit. Guess where that profit is going this year. To him. A million dollars. That's a turnaround. And by the way, we're still working with them. The temporary solution became a permanent one.

It can happen for you as well. Maybe not to that extreme, but you never know. You need to get your team in place. If you can't afford to hire a CFO, do an outsource one, and then bring it in-house if you think you're big enough where you need an in-house one.

Whoever you choose, make sure it's someone who knows your industry — someone who understands the numbers, the challenges, the risks and the rewards. Someone who is knowledgeable and reputable.

I hope this book answered your questions and gave you a roadmap for your company's future. If you still have questions, I'm always up for a conversation. Or, if you'd like to learn more about Virtual CFO's, I'm happy to have that talk as well. I just like to talk about accounting.

About the Author

As co-founder and CEO at Summit CPA Group, Jody Grunden offers more than 20 years of both public and corporate accounting experience.

Jody is a member of both the American Institute of Certified Public Accountants and the Indiana CPA Society and strongly believes that a well-run company will excel in both a good and bad economy. His firm was a recent recipient of the Indiana CPA Society's Innovation Award – an award given to a firm that embodies forward-thinking activities designed to address future issues and needs. Both Jody and Adam were recently recognized nationally by the American Institution of Certified Public Accountants (AICPA) for implementation of Innovative ideas. Because of their success, the firm has experienced significant growth over the past five years. Inc 5000 recently recognized Summit CPA Group as one of the fastest growing companies in the nation.

When he's not meeting with clients or team members, he's a nice guy who likes hockey, golf, and his family. Jody graduated from Indiana University's Kelley School of Business and would be remiss without at least one "Go Hoosiers!" reference somewhere in this book.

About the Summit CPA Group

Jody Grunden is the co-founder and CEO at Summit CPA Group. Founded in 2002, Summit CPA Group offers flat-fee Virtual CFO services helping clients maximize profits, minimize taxes, and increase cash flow for creative service professionals all over North America.

Unlike many others in the business of accounting who focus on historic financial statements and tax returns, Summit CPA Group operates under a profit-focused model, using dynamic forecasting models and key performance indicators with their clients to help them transcend their focus from simply "being in the black" to longer-term financial health and wealth.

Building on their foundation, Summit CPA Group started another line of business in 2010 –401K Audits. Since then, the Audit team has grown to be recognized as one of the top 5% of all firms performing that type of audit (based on quantity of audits). With the mission statement, *"Changing the way people think about accounting,"* the next big step for the Summit CPA will be helping make this level of service a norm rather than an exception within other accounting firms.

Made in the USA
Middletown, DE
09 February 2018